9/18

ground beef microwave meals

microwave cooking library®

by barbara methven

microwave cooking library®

For years, ground beef has been a staple of the American diet. Although eating styles have changed, cooks still prepare ground beef regularly, not only because it is economical and nutritious, but because the family enjoys it.

Many households keep a supply of ground beef in the freezer. Quickly defrosted in the microwave oven and combined with staples from the refrigerator and pantry, ground beef makes an ideal basic ingredient for last-minute easy meals.

Barbara Methven

Barbara Methven

CREDITS:
Design & Production: Cy DeCosse Incorporated
Art Director: Delores Swanson
Project Director: Peggy Ramette
Project Manager: Lisa Bergerud
Home Economists: Peggy Ramette, Ann Stuart
Assistant Home Economist: Sue Brue
Dietitian: Patricia D. Godfrey. R.D.
Consultants: Diane McCroskey Phillips, Grace Wells
Editors: Janice Cauley, Bernice Maehren
Production Director: Jim Bindas
Assistant Production Managers: Julie Churchill, Amelia Merz
Typesetting: Kevin D. Frakes, Linda Schloegel
Production Staff: Joe Fahey, Melissa Grabanski, Jim Huntley, Mark Jacobson, Yelena Konrardy, Daniel Meyers, Greg Wallace, Nik Wogstad
Studio Manager: Rebecca DaWald
Photographers: Rex Irmen, Tony Kubat, John Lauenstein, Bill Lindner, Mark Macemon, Mette Nielsen, Cathleen Shannon
Food Stylists: Sue Brue, Bobbette Destiche
Color Separations: Scantrans
Printing: R. R. Donnelley & Sons (0890)

Additional volumes in the Microwave Cooking Library series are available from the publisher:

- Basic Microwaving
- Recipe Conversion for Microwave
- Microwaving Meats
- Microwave Baking & Desserts
- Microwaving Meals in 30 Minutes
- Microwaving on a Diet
- Microwaving Fruits & Vegetables
- Microwaving Convenience Foods
- Microwaving for Holidays & Parties
- Microwaving for One & Two
- The Microwave & Freezer
- 101 Microwaving Secrets
- Microwaving Light & Healthy
- Microwaving Poultry & Seafood
- Microwaving America's Favorites
- Microwaving Fast & Easy Main Dishes
- More Microwaving Secrets
- Microwaving Light Meals & Snacks
- Holiday Microwave Ideas
- Easy Microwave Menus
- Low-fat Microwave Meals
- Cool Quick Summer Microwaving

CY DE COSSE INCORPORATED
Chairman: Cy DeCosse
President: James B. Maus
Executive Vice President: William B. Jones

Library of Congress Cataloging-in-Publication Data

Methven, Barbara.
  Ground beef microwave meals / by Barbara Methven.

    p. cm. — (Microwave cooking library)

  ISBN 0-86573-569-7 :
  1. Cookery (Beef) 2. Microwave cookery. I. Title. II. Series.
TX749.5.B43M47   1990
641.6'62 — dc20   90-32951
                                                              CIP

Contents

What You Need to Know Before You Start

Ground Beef Microwave Meals provides a fresh approach to ground beef. The recipes reflect contemporary preferences for the fresh color, texture and low sodium content of fresh or frozen produce rather than canned ingredients. They minimize cutting, chopping and other time-consuming procedures. Some recipes call for instant minced garlic or onion to save time, but fresh ingredients can always be substituted.

This is not a diet book. The contemporary main dishes and modern versions of old favorites are nutritionally sound and most meet recent recommendations for protein, carbohydrate, fat and sodium levels. Where ground beef is the only protein source, recipes call for one pound to serve four persons.

Some dishes may be even more economical than the casseroles of the past. When ground beef is combined with supplementary protein sources, such as rice, beans, pasta or cheese, recipes call for one-half pound to meet the protein requirements of four people.

Combinations of ground beef and complex carbohydrates such as rice, pasta or beans can be found in the traditional cuisine of many nations. The ground beef supplies amino acids necessary for complete protein and sound nutrition. In addition, beef provides an excellent source of iron and B vitamins.

The information contained in this introductory section was provided by the Beef Industry Council of the National Live Stock and Meat Board.

What About Fat?

Ground beef needs some fat for juiciness and flavor. Although no national labeling standards apply to beef that is ground and packaged in supermarkets, the USDA regulations require that prepackaged regular ground beef contain no more than 30% fat (that is, almost one-third of each pound can be fat). Most regular ground beef contains about 73% lean and 27% fat. Lean ground beef is approximately 80% lean and 20% fat. Extra-lean ground beef tends to be 85% lean and 15% fat. Labels stating the percentage of lean are more accurate than labels marked only regular, lean or extra-lean.

Although lean and extra-lean ground beef cost a little more, you get more meat and more protein per pound. When cooked to medium, a pound of regular ground beef yields 73.20 grams of protein, compared to 80.14 grams for lean and 84.73 grams for extra-lean.

Fat and juices from regular, lean and extra-lean ground beef are drained into measures after beef is microwaved until no longer pink (for easier comparison, drippings in photo have been refrigerated to solidify fat). Some fat still remains in meat. Cooking extracts about one ounce more fat and juices from regular ground beef (left) than it does from extra-lean (right).

The recipes in this book were developed and tested using 80% lean ground beef. If you need to reduce fat content further, you may substitute extra-lean beef. Take care when using 85% lean beef to avoid compacting or overcooking it. If you substitute regular ground beef for lean in these recipes, drain the fat after the initial microwaving, before adding other ingredients.

Nutritional Information

Following each recipe, a nutritional analysis provides the per serving measurement of calories, protein, carbohydrate, fat, cholesterol and sodium. The analysis also includes exchanges, which indicate the source and balance of a food's calories. Where a recipe makes a flexible number of servings, such as four to six, the analysis is based on the greater number of servings. Optional ingredients are not included in the nutritional analysis.

Buying & Storing Ground Beef

Take extra care when selecting and storing ground beef. Grinding exposes more cut surface to bacteria, which can cause spoilage, so ground beef is more perishable than solid pieces of meat.

When grocery shopping, pick up your ground beef just before you head for the checkout counter. Take it straight home and refrigerate it immediately. The refrigerator temperature should be under 40°F.

Some supermarkets mark prepackaged ground beef with either the packaging date or a "use before" date, which can help you choose the freshest beef. Color is also a guide to quality. Since meat turns bright red when exposed to air, the surface of ground beef generally looks red, while the interior may be a dull brown. When you divide ground beef at home, the interior should brighten. Beef that remains brown after exposure to air is not fresh. Return it to the store.

Choose packaged ground beef that feels cold. Check for freshness date and avoid torn packages. Refrigerate ground beef, sealed in plastic film, up to two days. Meat wrapped in unwaxed butcher's paper should be repackaged in plastic film or aluminum foil. Meat may be divided into smaller portions.

Freezing & Defrosting Ground Beef

You can freeze ground beef packaged in super-market wrap for a week or two. For longer storage, repackage the meat in freezer wrap, heavy-duty foil or freezer-weight plastic food-storage bags. Repackaged ground beef can be kept for three months in a freezer at 0°F.

To maintain quality, defrost ground beef just before cooking. The defrosting chart below is for 50%

(Medium) power. Many microwave ovens have a special defrost setting, which varies from 30% to 50% power, depending on the make of oven.

Lower power settings take more time, but produce more even results. To use a defrost setting, follow the method illustrated here and consult your use and care manual for total time.

How to Freeze Ground Beef

Wrap ground beef airtight for freezing. Air trapped inside the package draws moisture from the meat, forming ice crystals that leave dry patches of freezer burn.

Divide ground beef into recipe-size portions before freezing. Many recipes in this book call for ½ pound of ground beef. Flat portions defrost more quickly and evenly than bulky packages.

Form ground beef into patties for burgers. Gently shape into even rounds, keeping the edges as thick as the centers. Stack patties, separated by layers of wax paper and wrap for the freezer.

How to Defrost Ground Beef

Unwrap ground beef and place meat in 2-quart casserole. Microwave for one-third the total defrosting time. Remove defrosted meat and microwave remaining meat for second one-third of time.

Remove defrosted meat, break up remaining ground beef and microwave for final one-third of time. Let stand for 5 to 10 minutes to complete defrosting, if necessary.

Defrosting Chart

Amount	50% (Medium)
1 lb.	3 to 5 min.
½ lb.	2 to 4 min.
2 patties (¼ lb. each)	3 to 5 min.
4 patties (¼ lb. each)	4 to 6 min.

Use two forks to mix ground beef with other ingredients for meatloaves and meatballs.

Preparing Ground Beef

Handle ground beef gently. If you overwork and compact ground beef, the protein binds tightly, making a dense and firm product. Overhandling results in hard meatballs or hamburgers that are tough. Take special care when using 85% lean ground beef.

Wet your hands before shaping meatballs, so ground beef will not cling to your palms. When preparing meatloaf, gently pat the mixture into a loaf shape and set it into the dish so there is space around the sides. Avoid pressing the meat into the baking dish.

Two Ways to Microwave Grease-free Ground Beef

Crumble 1 lb. ground beef into microwave-safe plastic collander set over 2-quart casserole. Microwave at High for 4 to 7 minutes, or until meat is no longer pink, stirring 1 or 2 times during cooking to break apart. Fat and juices drain into casserole. Discard.

Layer 4 paper towels in 2-quart casserole. Crumble 1 lb. ground beef over towels. Microwave at High for 4 to 7 minutes, or until meat is no longer pink, stirring 1 or 2 times during cooking to break apart. Lift one side of paper towels, so ground beef falls into casserole. Discard towels, which have absorbed fat and juices, and proceed with recipe.

Tips for Preparing Hamburgers

Microwave hamburgers for a juicy, meaty taste. They do not develop a brown crust like conventionally grilled or fried burgers, although they brown slightly during standing time (left). Once the patty is encased in a bun, browning becomes unimportant. To add flavor and color to patties, brush them with Worcestershire, soy, teriyaki or barbecue sauce before microwaving (right).

Grill extra patties when you barbecue hamburgers over charcoal. Layer cooked, cooled patties with wax paper; stack, wrap in foil and freeze. Microwave hamburgers later for just-grilled flavor.

Defrost and heat in one step. Unwrap 1 or 2 cooked, frozen burgers and place on plate. Microwave 1 burger at 50% (Medium) for 1¼ to 4 minutes, or until hot, turning over after half the time. Microwave 2 burgers at 50% (Medium) for 2½ to 8 minutes, or until hot, turning over after half the time.

Skewered Greek Meatballs
with Yogurt Dipping Sauce

◄ Skewered Greek Meatballs with Yogurt Dipping Sauce

Sauce:
- 1 carton (8 oz.) plain low-fat yogurt
- 2 tablespoons seeded chopped cucumber
- 1 teaspoon lemon juice
- ½ teaspoon dried mint flakes
- ¼ teaspoon garlic powder

Meatballs:
- 1 lb. lean ground beef, crumbled
- ⅓ cup unseasoned dry bread crumbs
- 1 egg
- ¼ teaspoon garlic powder
- ¼ teaspoon salt

Marinade:
- ¼ cup olive oil
- 2 tablespoons lemon juice
- 1 teaspoon dried mint flakes
- 1 teaspoon dried oregano leaves

- 24 wooden skewers (6-inch)
- 6 cucumber slices (¾-inch), cut into quarters
- 24 cherry tomatoes

12 servings

In small mixing bowl, combine all sauce ingredients. Mix well. Set aside.

In medium mixing bowl, combine all meatball ingredients. Mix well. Shape into 24 meatballs, about 1¼ inches in diameter. Arrange meatballs in 2-quart casserole. Set aside.

In 1-cup measure, combine all marinade ingredients. Mix well. Pour marinade over meatballs. Cover. Chill about 1 hour, stirring gently to rearrange meatballs once.

Drain. Cover with wax paper. Microwave at High for 5 to 8 minutes, or until meatballs are firm and no longer pink, stirring gently to rearrange twice.

On each wooden skewer, thread 1 meatball, 1 cucumber quarter and 1 cherry tomato. Serve skewered meatballs with sauce.

Per Serving:			
Calories:	118	Cholesterol:	48 mg.
Protein:	9 g.	Sodium:	107 mg.
Carbohydrate:	5 g.	Exchanges:	1 medium-fat meat, 1 vegetable,
Fat:	7 g.		½ fat

◄ Chinese-style Meatballs

Meatballs:
- 1 lb. lean ground beef, crumbled
- ⅓ cup unseasoned dry bread crumbs
- 1 egg
- ½ teaspoon dry mustard
- ½ teaspoon ground ginger
- ¼ teaspoon garlic powder
- ¼ teaspoon salt

Sauce:
- ¾ cup catsup
- ½ cup honey
- ¼ cup soy sauce

Sliced green onions (optional)

8 servings

In medium mixing bowl, combine all meatball ingredients. Mix well. Shape into 24 meatballs, about 1¼ inches in diameter. Arrange meatballs in 2-quart casserole. Cover with wax paper. Microwave at High for 5 to 8 minutes, or until meatballs are firm and no longer pink, stirring gently to rearrange twice. Drain. Set aside.

In small mixing bowl, combine all sauce ingredients. Mix well. Pour sauce over meatballs. Stir to coat meatballs with sauce. Re-cover with wax paper. Microwave at High for 3 to 5 minutes, or until meatballs and sauce are hot, stirring gently to rearrange once or twice. Sprinkle with onions. Serve with wooden picks.

Per Serving:			
Calories:	233	Cholesterol:	70 mg.
Protein:	12 g.	Sodium:	923 mg.
Carbohydrate:	28 g.	Exchanges:	1½ starch, 1 medium-fat meat,
Fat:	8 g.		1 vegetable, ½ fat

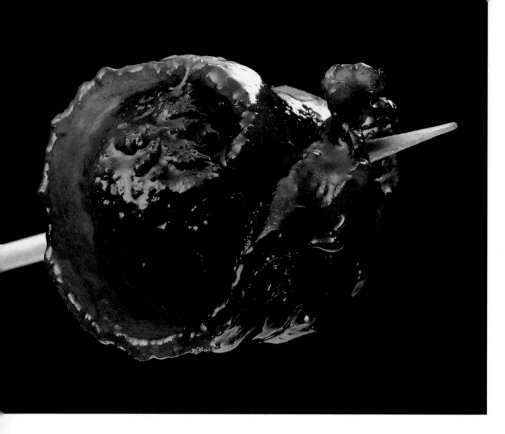

Meatball Wrap-ups ▲

12	slices bacon	2	tablespoons vegetable oil
½	lb. lean ground beef, crumbled	2	tablespoons soy sauce
1	egg	2	tablespoons white vinegar
¼	cup unseasoned dry bread crumbs	2	tablespoons catsup
1	teaspoon dried parsley flakes	2	tablespoons honey
		¼	teaspoon garlic powder

12 servings

Layer 3 paper towels on plate. Arrange 6 bacon slices on paper towels. Top with 3 more paper towels and the remaining bacon. Cover with 1 paper towel. Microwave at High for 6 to 8 minutes, or just until bacon begins to brown and is slightly cooked. Set aside.

In medium mixing bowl, combine ground beef, egg, bread crumbs and parsley. Mix well. Shape into 24 meatballs, about 1 inch in diameter.

Cut each bacon slice in half crosswise. Wrap each meatball with 1 bacon piece. Secure with wooden pick. Arrange meatballs in single layer in 8-inch square baking dish. Set aside.

In 2-cup measure, combine remaining ingredients. Mix well. Pour over meatballs. Cover with plastic wrap. Chill ½ hour, rearranging once.

Arrange meatballs on roasting rack. Microwave at High for 5 to 7 minutes, or until meatballs are firm and no longer pink, rotating rack and rearranging meatballs once or twice.

Per Serving:			
Calories:	97	Cholesterol:	40 mg.
Protein:	6 g.	Sodium:	182 mg.
Carbohydrate:	3 g.	Exchanges:	1 medium-fat meat, ½ vegetable
Fat:	7 g.		

Texas-style Barbecue Meatballs

Meatballs:

1	lb. lean ground beef, crumbled
⅓	cup unseasoned dry bread crumbs
1	egg
1	tablespoon dried parsley flakes
2	teaspoons Worcestershire sauce

Sauce:

1	cup barbecue sauce
1	cup chili sauce
¼	cup packed brown sugar
¼	cup red wine vinegar
1	tablespoon dry mustard
¼	teaspoon crushed red pepper flakes

8 servings

In medium mixing bowl, combine all meatball ingredients. Mix well. Shape into 24 meatballs, about 1¼ inches in diameter. Arrange meatballs in 2-quart casserole. Cover with wax paper. Microwave at High for 5 to 8 minutes, or until meatballs are firm and no longer pink, stirring gently to rearrange twice. Drain. Set aside.

In 4-cup measure, combine all sauce ingredients. Mix well. Pour sauce over meatballs. Stir to coat meatballs with sauce. Re-cover with wax paper. Microwave at High for 4 to 6 minutes, or until meatballs and sauce are hot, stirring once or twice. Serve with wooden picks.

Per Serving:	
Calories:	225
Protein:	13 g.
Carbohydrate:	23 g.
Fat:	9 g.
Cholesterol:	70 mg.
Sodium:	798 mg.
Exchanges:	½ starch, 1 medium-fat meat, 3 vegetable, 1 fat

Taco Scoop Supreme

- 1 lb. lean ground beef, crumbled
- 1 pkg. (1.25 oz.) taco seasoning mix
- ¼ cup water
- 1 pkg. (3 oz.) cream cheese
- 1 pkg. (6 oz.) frozen avocado guacamole, defrosted
- ½ cup sour cream
- 1 cup shredded lettuce
- ½ cup seeded chopped tomato
- 2 tablespoons sliced black olives
- 2 tablespoons sliced green onions
  Tortilla chips

8 to 10 servings

In 2-quart casserole, microwave ground beef at High for 4 to 7 minutes, or until meat is no longer pink, stirring twice to break apart. Drain. Add seasoning mix and water. Mix well. Microwave at High for 2 to 4 minutes, or until liquid is absorbed and mixture is slightly thickened, stirring twice. Spoon meat mixture evenly into 10-inch deep-dish pie plate. Set aside.

In medium mixing bowl, microwave cream cheese at High for 15 to 30 seconds, or until softened. Add guacamole and sour cream. Mix well. Spread guacamole mixture evenly over meat mixture. Sprinkle with lettuce, tomato, olives and onions. Serve immediately with tortilla chips.

Per Serving:	
Calories:	180
Protein:	10 g.
Carbohydrate:	4 g.
Fat:	14 g.
Cholesterol:	43 mg.
Sodium:	237 mg.
Exchanges:	1 medium-fat meat, 1 vegetable, 1½ fat

Crispy Taco Puff ▲

- 1 sheet frozen puff pastry, defrosted (half of 17¼ oz. package)
- 1 pkg. (8 oz.) cream cheese
- 1 lb. lean ground beef, crumbled
- 1 pkg. (1.25 oz.) taco seasoning mix
- ¼ cup water
- 1 cup shredded Cheddar cheese
- 1 cup shredded lettuce
- 1 cup seeded chopped tomato

30 servings

Heat conventional oven to 350°F. Defrost pastry at room temperature for about 20 minutes. Unfold pastry. Place on lightly floured board. Roll into 14 × 11-inch rectangle. Place rectangle on large baking sheet. Prick generously with fork. Bake for 5 minutes. If center puffs, prick with fork until pastry deflates. Bake for 10 to 15 minutes longer, or until light golden brown. Cool completely.

In small mixing bowl, microwave cream cheese at 50% (Medium) for 1½ to 3 minutes, or until softened. Spread cream cheese evenly over cooled pastry to within ½ inch of edge. Set aside.

In 2-quart casserole, microwave ground beef at High for 4 to 7 minutes, or until meat is no longer pink, stirring twice to break apart. Drain. Add seasoning mix and water. Mix well. Microwave at High for 2 to 4 minutes, or until liquid is absorbed and mixture is slightly thickened, stirring twice.

Spoon mixture evenly over cream cheese. Sprinkle evenly with cheese, lettuce and tomato. Cut into thirty 2-inch squares.

Per Serving:			
Calories:	105	Cholesterol:	22 mg.
Protein:	5 g.	Sodium:	105 mg.
Carbohydrate:	3 g.	Exchanges:	1 vegetable, ½ medium-fat meat, 1 fat
Fat:	8 g.		

15

Savory Wonton Bundles ▲

2 tablespoons dry mustard
1 tablespoon plus 2 teaspoons water
½ lb. lean ground beef, crumbled
¼ cup sliced green onions
2 tablespoons soy sauce
1 tablespoon cornstarch
1 teaspoon five-spice powder
¼ teaspoon garlic powder
2 pkgs. (8 oz. each) refrigerated crescent roll dough
Oriental plum sauce

10 to 12 servings

Per Serving:	
Calories:	171
Protein:	6 g.
Carbohydrate:	18 g.
Fat:	8 g.
Cholesterol:	12 mg.
Sodium:	626 mg.
Exchanges:	1 starch,
	½ medium-fat meat,
	½ vegetable, 1 fat

How to Make Savory Wonton Bundles

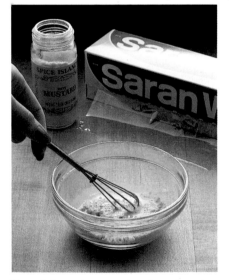

Combine dry mustard and water in small bowl. Mix well. Cover with plastic wrap. Set aside.

Combine ground beef, onions, soy sauce, cornstarch, five-spice powder and garlic powder in 1-quart casserole. Mix well. Microwave at High for 3 to 4½ minutes, or until no longer pink, stirring once to break apart. Set aside.

16

Sweet Hot Mini Cabbage Rolls

1 head cabbage (about 3 lbs.)

Meat Mixture:

½ lb. lean ground beef, crumbled
⅓ cup uncooked instant rice
1 egg
1 tablespoon instant minced onion
¼ teaspoon ground allspice
¼ teaspoon salt
⅛ teaspoon cayenne

Sauce:

1 can (10¾ oz.) condensed tomato soup
½ cup water
2 tablespoons packed brown sugar
¼ teaspoon ground allspice
⅛ teaspoon cayenne

12 servings

Remove core from cabbage. Rinse cabbage and shake out excess water. Wrap in plastic wrap. Microwave at High for 5 to 7 minutes, or until outer leaves soften. Let stand for 5 minutes.

Carefully remove 6 leaves. Wrap and refrigerate remaining cabbage for future use. Cut hard center rib from each leaf. Cut each leaf in half lengthwise. Set aside.

In small mixing bowl, combine all meat mixture ingredients. Mix well. Divide mixture into 12 equal portions. Place 1 portion on each leaf. Fold edges over and roll up, enclosing filling. Arrange cabbage rolls, seam-sides-down, in 2-quart casserole. Set aside.

In medium mixing bowl, combine all sauce ingredients. Mix well. Pour over cabbage rolls. Cover. Microwave at High for 6 to 11 minutes, or until rolls are firm and hot, stirring gently to rearrange rolls twice.

Per Serving:
Calories:	75	Cholesterol:	35 mg.
Protein:	4 g.	Sodium:	240 mg.
Carbohydrate:	7 g.	Exchanges:	½ medium-fat meat, 1½ vegetable,
Fat:	3 g.		½ fat

Heat conventional oven to 450°F. Remove crescent roll dough from 1 package. Place dough on lightly floured board. Press perforations to seal. Roll dough into 12 × 9-inch rectangle. Cut into twelve 3 × 3-inch squares.

Spoon 1 heaping teaspoon filling in center of each square. Fold bottom corner over filling to opposite corner, forming triangle. Press edges to seal. Bring long corners together. Overlap slightly; press to seal. Repeat with remaining dough and filling.

Arrange filled bundles on large ungreased baking sheet. Bake for 6 to 8 minutes, or until golden brown. Remove from pan to serving platter immediately. Serve warm with mustard sauce and plum sauce.

Layered Beef Quesadillas

1 cup chopped green pepper
1 cup chopped red pepper
2 tablespoons water
½ lb. lean ground beef, crumbled
¾ teaspoon chili powder
¼ teaspoon garlic powder
¼ teaspoon dried oregano leaves
¼ teaspoon salt
6 flour tortillas (8-inch)
2 cups shredded Co-Jack cheese

2 quesadillas
8 servings

In 2-quart casserole, combine peppers and water. Cover. Microwave at High for 2 to 3 minutes, or until peppers are tender-crisp, stirring once. Drain. Remove ¼ cup pepper mixture. Set aside.

Add ground beef to remaining peppers. Mix well. Microwave at High, uncovered, for 2 to 4 minutes, or until meat is no longer pink, stirring once to break apart. Drain. Add chili powder, garlic powder, oregano and salt. Mix well. Microwave at High, uncovered, for 1 to 3 minutes, or until mixture is hot and flavors are blended, stirring once.

Place 1 tortilla on 10-inch plate. Sprinkle with one-fourth of meat mixture and ¼ cup cheese. Repeat layers once, ending with flour tortilla. Sprinkle with ½ cup cheese and 2 tablespoons reserved pepper mixture. Repeat with remaining ingredients.

Microwave each quesadilla at 70% (Medium High) for 2½ to 3 minutes, or until cheese is melted, rotating plate once. Cut into 8 equal pieces. Serve topped with salsa, if desired.

Per Serving:			
Calories:	218	Cholesterol:	43 mg.
Protein:	13 g.	Sodium:	237 mg.
Carbohydrate:	12 g.	Exchanges:	½ starch, 1½ medium-fat meat,
Fat:	13 g.		1 vegetable, 1 fat

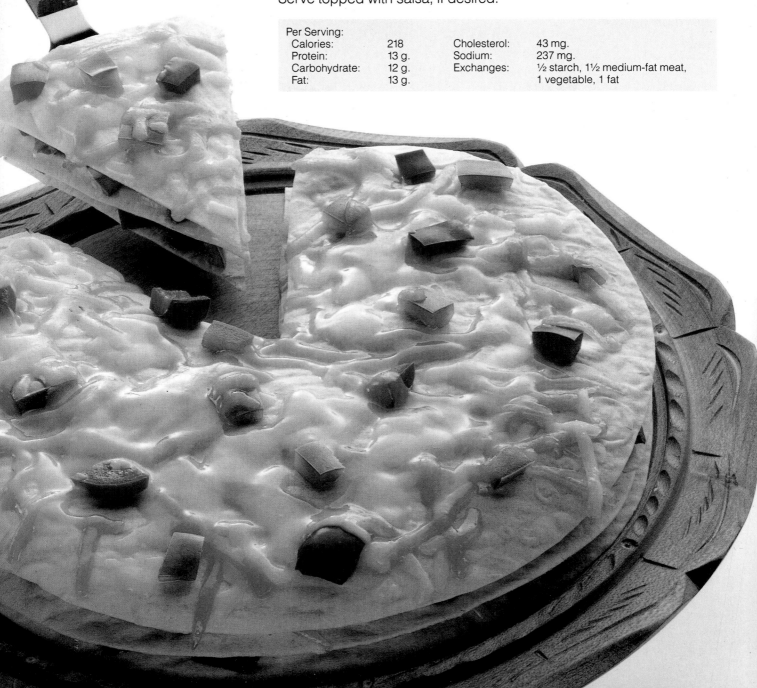

Oriental Appetizer Platter

1 pkg. (8 oz.) cream cheese
½ lb. lean ground beef,
   crumbled
¼ cup water
2 tablespoons packed brown
   sugar
2 tablespoons soy sauce
2 tablespoons catsup
1 tablespoon lemon juice
2 teaspoons cornstarch
¼ teaspoon garlic powder
¼ teaspoon ground ginger
¼ teaspoon crushed red
   pepper flakes
½ cup shredded carrot
¼ cup plus 2 tablespoons
   sliced green onions, divided
¼ cup canned sliced water
   chestnuts, chopped
2 tablespoons cashew pieces
   Assorted crackers

6 to 8 servings

In small mixing bowl, microwave cream cheese at 50% (Medium) for 1½ to 3 minutes, or until softened. On 12-inch platter, spread cream cheese to within 2 inches of edge. Set aside.

In 1-quart casserole, microwave ground beef at High for 2 to 4 minutes, or until meat is no longer pink, stirring once to break apart. Drain.

Add water, sugar, soy sauce, catsup, lemon juice, cornstarch, garlic powder, ginger and red pepper flakes. Mix well. Microwave at High for 4 to 6 minutes, or until mixture is thickened and translucent, stirring twice.

Add carrot, ¼ cup onions and water chestnuts. Mix well. Spoon mixture evenly over cream cheese to within ½ inch of edge. Sprinkle top with remaining 2 tablespoons onions and the cashew pieces. Serve with assorted crackers.

Per Serving:			
Calories:	199	Cholesterol:	49 mg.
Protein:	8 g.	Sodium:	406 mg.
Carbohydrate:	9 g.	Exchanges:	½ medium-fat meat,
Fat:	15 g.		2 vegetable, 2½ fat

Pizza Pull-aparts ▶

½ lb. lean ground beef, crumbled
¼ cup chopped green pepper
¼ cup chopped onion
¼ cup chopped pimiento-stuffed green olives
2 tablespoons catsup
¼ cup margarine or butter
1 teaspoon Italian seasoning
⅛ teaspoon garlic powder
2 pkgs. (7.5 oz. each) refrigerated buttermilk biscuits
   Spaghetti sauce

8 to 10 servings

Per Serving:
Calories: 226
Protein: 8 g.
Carbohydrate: 23 g.
Fat: 11 g.
Cholesterol: 14 mg.
Sodium: 658 mg.
Exchanges: 1 starch,
                1½ vegetable, 2 fat

How to Make Pizza Pull-aparts

Heat conventional oven to 350°F. In 1-quart casserole, combine ground beef, pepper and onion. Cover. Microwave at High for 3 to 4 minutes, or until meat is no longer pink, stirring once to break apart. Drain. Add olives and catsup. Mix well. Set aside.

Melt margarine at High for 1¼ to 1½ minutes in small mixing bowl. Add Italian seasoning and garlic powder. Mix well. Set aside. Remove biscuits from packages. Using fingers, stretch each biscuit to 3-inch diameter. Dredge biscuits in margarine mixture.

Place 1 heaping tablespoon meat mixture in center of each biscuit. Fold biscuit in half, enclosing filling. Do not seal edges. Stand filling-side-up against side of 8-inch round cake pan.

Southwestern-style Cheese Dip

½ lb. lean ground beef,
   crumbled
½ cup chopped green pepper
½ cup chopped red pepper
2 tablespoons canned
   chopped green chilies

1 can (15 oz.) chili beans in chili
   gravy, undrained
1 lb. pasteurized process
   cheese loaf with jalapeño
   pepper, cut into 1-inch cubes
Tortilla chips

16 servings

In 2-quart casserole, combine ground beef, peppers and chilies. Mix well. Microwave at High for 4 to 6 minutes, or until meat is no longer pink and peppers are tender, stirring twice to break apart. Drain.

Add remaining ingredients, except tortilla chips. Cover. Microwave at 50% (Medium) for 9 to 13 minutes, or until cheese is melted, stirring 2 or 3 times. Serve with tortilla chips.

Per Serving:			
Calories:	134	Cholesterol:	24 mg.
Protein:	9 g.	Sodium:	482 mg.
Carbohydrate:	7 g.	Exchanges:	½ starch, 1 medium-fat meat, ½ fat
Fat:	8 g.		

Repeat with remaining biscuits, arranging in slightly overlapping concentric circles, filling pan. Bake for 35 to 40 minutes, or until biscuits are golden brown. Loosen edges and remove to serving platter. Serve with spaghetti sauce for dipping.

Beef & Feta Triangles

½ lb. lean ground beef,
    crumbled
½ cup crumbled feta cheese
¼ cup sliced green onions
¼ cup snipped fresh parsley
2 teaspoons dried dill weed
⅓ cup margarine or butter
9 sheets frozen phyllo dough
    (17 × 12-inch), defrosted

9 servings

Per Serving:	
Calories:	155
Protein:	6 g.
Carbohydrate:	6 g.
Fat:	12 g.
Cholesterol:	22 mg.
Sodium:	233 mg.
Exchanges:	½ starch, 1 medium-fat meat, 1 fat

How to Make Beef & Feta Triangles

Heat conventional oven to 400°F. In 1-quart casserole, microwave ground beef at High for 2 to 4 minutes, or until meat is no longer pink, stirring once to break apart. Drain.

Add cheese, onions, parsley and dill weed. Mix well. Set aside. In small bowl, microwave margarine at High for 1½ to 1¾ minutes, or until melted. Set aside.

Unroll and remove phyllo sheets. Cover with plastic wrap. Working quickly, fold 1 sheet lengthwise in half. Cut lengthwise into 2 strips. Brush lightly with melted margarine.

Place 1 tablespoon of meat mixture in corner of strip and fold to form triangle. Continue folding to end of strip, keeping triangle shape. Brush top with melted margarine.

Place on large ungreased baking sheet. Repeat with remaining phyllo and filling. Bake for 15 to 17 minutes, or until golden brown. Serve warm.

Savory Stuffed ▶ Mushrooms

- 8 large fresh mushrooms (1½ to 2-inch diameter)
- ¼ lb. lean ground beef, crumbled
- ¼ teaspoon fennel seed, crushed
- ⅛ to ¼ teaspoon crushed red pepper flakes
- 2 tablespoons unseasoned dry bread crumbs
- 2 teaspoons dried parsley flakes
- ¼ teaspoon garlic powder
- ¼ teaspoon salt
- 2 slices (¾ oz. each) pasteurized process American cheese, each cut into quarters

6 to 8 servings

Remove stems from mushrooms. Set caps aside. Finely chop stems to yield ⅓ cup. Set aside. Reserve remaining stems for future use.

In 1-quart casserole, mix ground beef, fennel and red pepper flakes. Microwave at High for 2 to 3 minutes, or until meat is no longer pink, stirring once to break apart. Drain.

Add chopped stems, bread crumbs, parsley, garlic powder and salt. Mix well. Spoon mixture evenly into mushroom caps, mounding slightly.

Arrange on serving plate. Cover with wax paper. Microwave at 50% (Medium) for 6 to 11 minutes, or until mushrooms are hot and tender, rotating plate twice. Top mushrooms with cheese slice quarters. Let stand for 5 minutes, or until cheese is melted.

Per Serving:	
Calories:	56
Protein:	4 g.
Carbohydrate:	2 g.
Fat:	4 g.
Cholesterol:	14 mg.
Sodium:	163 mg.
Exchanges:	½ medium-fat meat, ½ vegetable, ½ fat

Mini Swiss & Caraway Meat Pies

- 1 pkg. (10 oz.) flaky refrigerated biscuits
- ½ lb. lean ground beef, crumbled
- ½ teaspoon caraway seed
- ¾ cup finely shredded Swiss cheese
- 1 tablespoon plus 1 teaspoon sweet hot mustard
- 1 teaspoon dried parsley flakes
- ¼ teaspoon salt

8 to 10 servings

Lightly grease 20 miniature muffin cups. Remove biscuits from package. Separate each biscuit into 2 pieces. Line each muffin cup with 1 biscuit piece, pressing gently up sides of cups. Set aside.

Heat conventional oven to 450°F. In 1-quart casserole, combine ground beef and caraway seed. Microwave at High for 2 to 4 minutes, or until meat is no longer pink, stirring once to break apart. Drain. Add remaining ingredients. Mix well.

Spoon mixture evenly into centers of lined muffin cups, mounding slightly and pressing gently to pack. Bake for 10 to 12 minutes, or until golden brown. Remove from cups. Serve warm.

Per Serving:			
Calories:	168	Cholesterol:	22 mg.
Protein:	8 g.	Sodium:	413 mg.
Carbohydrate:	13 g.	Exchanges:	1 starch, ½ medium-fat meat, 1 fat
Fat:	9 g.		

Salads

Pepper Beef & Pasta Salad

Ginger Beef & Orange Salad

¼ cup frozen orange juice
    concentrate, defrosted
½ cup vegetable oil, divided
2 tablespoons red wine vinegar
8 wonton skins (3½-inch
    square)
½ lb. lean ground beef,
    crumbled
1 egg
2 tablespoons unseasoned dry
    bread crumbs
1 teaspoon soy sauce
¼ teaspoon garlic powder
¼ teaspoon ground ginger
1 cup fresh snow pea pods
2 tablespoons water
8 cups Bibb lettuce, torn into
    bite-size pieces
1 can (11 oz.) mandarin orange
    segments, drained

4 servings

In 1-cup measure, combine orange juice concentrate, ¼ cup oil and the vinegar. Mix well. Set aside.

Cut wonton skins into thin strips. Heat remaining ¼ cup oil in 10-inch skillet conventionally over medium-high heat. Drop strips by small hand-fuls into hot oil. Fry until light golden brown, about 30 seconds, tossing gently. Remove with slotted spoon. Drain on paper towels. Repeat with remaining strips. Set aside.

In medium mixing bowl, combine ground beef, egg, bread crumbs, soy sauce, garlic powder and ginger. Mix well. Shape into 16 meatballs, about ¾ inch in diameter. Arrange meatballs in single layer in 8-inch square baking dish. Microwave at High for 3 to 4 minutes, or until meat-balls are firm and no longer pink, rearranging once. Drain. Set aside.

In 1-quart casserole, combine pea pods and water. Cover. Microwave at High for 1 to 3 minutes, or until pea pods are very hot and color brightens, stirring once. Rinse with cold water. Drain.

On 12-inch platter, arrange lettuce, mandarin orange segments, wonton strips, meatballs and pea pods. Garnish with fresh enoki mushrooms, if desired. Serve with dressing.

Per Serving:			
Calories:	432	Cholesterol:	104 mg.
Protein:	16 g.	Sodium:	266 mg.
Carbohydrate:	25 g.	Exchanges:	½ starch, 2 medium-fat meat,
Fat:	31 g.		½ vegetable, 1 fruit, 4 fat

Meatball & Fettucini Salad

8 oz. uncooked fettucini, broken into 2-inch lengths
1 pkg. (16 oz.) frozen broccoli, cauliflower and carrots
¼ cup water

Dressing:

⅓ cup olive oil
2 tablespoons white wine vinegar
¼ teaspoon dried basil leaves
¼ teaspoon salt
⅛ teaspoon garlic powder
⅛ teaspoon crushed red pepper flakes

Meatballs:

½ lb. lean ground beef, crumbled
1 egg
¼ cup unseasoned dry bread crumbs
¼ teaspoon dried basil leaves
⅛ teaspoon garlic powder

¼ cup grated Parmesan cheese
¼ cup snipped fresh parsley

4 servings

Prepare fettucini as directed on package. Rinse and drain. Place in large mixing bowl or salad bowl. Set aside.

In 2-quart casserole, combine vegetables and water. Cover. Microwave at High for 7 to 9 minutes, or until vegetables are defrosted, stirring once. Drain. Add to cooked fettucini.

In 1-cup measure, combine all dressing ingredients. Mix well. Add to vegetable mixture.

In medium mixing bowl, combine all meatball ingredients. Shape into 16 meatballs, about ¾ inch in diameter. Arrange meatballs in single layer in 8-inch square baking dish. Microwave at High for 3 to 4 minutes, or until meatballs are firm and no longer pink, rearranging once. Drain.

Add meatballs to vegetable mixture. Add cheese and parsley. Toss to combine. Serve immediately.

Per Serving:			
Calories:	530	Cholesterol:	109 mg.
Protein:	24 g.	Sodium:	379 mg.
Carbohydrate:	59 g.	Exchanges:	3 starch, 1½ medium-fat meat,
Fat:	22 g.		3 vegetable, 3 fat

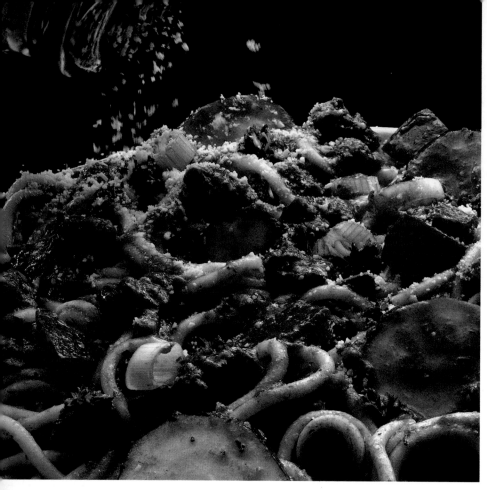

Hot Spaghetti-Beef Salad

◄ **Hot Spaghetti-Beef Salad**

- 8 oz. uncooked spaghetti
- 1 medium tomato, seeded and cut into chunks
- 1 cup thinly sliced zucchini
- ½ cup sliced green onions
- ¼ cup snipped fresh parsley
- 1 lb. lean ground beef, crumbled
- 1 can (8 oz.) tomato sauce
- 2 tablespoons olive or vegetable oil
- 1 tablespoon red wine vinegar
- 1 teaspoon Italian seasoning
- ½ teaspoon sugar
- ¼ teaspoon garlic powder
- ¼ teaspoon crushed red pepper flakes
- ¼ teaspoon salt

6 to 8 servings

Prepare spaghetti as directed on package. Rinse and drain. Place in large mixing bowl or salad bowl. Add tomato, zucchini, onions and parsley. Mix well. Set aside.

In 2-quart casserole, microwave ground beef at High for 4 to 7 minutes, or until meat is no longer pink, stirring twice to break apart. Drain. Add remaining ingredients. Mix well.

Microwave at High, uncovered, for 5 to 8 minutes, or until mixture is hot and flavors are blended, stirring twice. Add to spaghetti mixture. Toss to coat. Serve immediately. Sprinkle with grated Parmesan cheese, if desired.

Per Serving:	
Calories:	262
Protein:	14 g.
Carbohydrate:	26 g.
Fat:	11 g.
Cholesterol:	35 mg.
Sodium:	273 mg.
Exchanges:	1 starch, 1 medium-fat meat, 2 vegetable, 1 fat

Tangy Taco Salad

- 1 lb. lean ground beef, crumbled
- 1 pkg. (1.25 oz.) taco seasoning mix
- ¼ cup water
- 8 cups torn leaf lettuce
- 2 cups seeded chopped tomatoes
- 2 cups shredded Cheddar cheese
- 1 cup sliced black olives
- 2 cups crushed tortilla chips
- ½ cup Russian or western salad dressing
- ½ cup taco sauce

6 to 8 servings

In 2-quart casserole, microwave ground beef at High for 4 to 7 minutes, or until no longer pink, stirring twice to break apart. Drain.

Add seasoning mix and water. Mix well. Microwave at High for 2 to 4 minutes, or until liquid is absorbed and mixture is slightly thickened, stirring twice. Set mixture aside to cool slightly.

In large mixing bowl or salad bowl, combine lettuce, tomatoes, cheese, olives and tortilla chips. Toss to combine.

In small mixing bowl, combine dressing and taco sauce. Mix well. Add ground beef and dressing mixture to lettuce mixture. Toss to combine. Serve immediately.

Per Serving:			
Calories:	415	Cholesterol:	67 mg.
Protein:	20 g.	Sodium:	772 mg.
Carbohydrate:	17 g.	Exchanges:	½ starch, 2 medium-fat meat, 2 vegetable, 4 fat
Fat:	30 g.		

Santa Fe Salad

1 pkg. (5.6 oz.) refrigerated taco salad shells (4 shells)

Dressing:

¼ cup olive oil
2 tablespoons lime juice
¼ teaspoon dried cilantro leaves
¼ teaspoon cumin seed
¼ teaspoon garlic powder

½ lb. lean ground beef, crumbled
1 teaspoon lime juice
½ teaspoon paprika
½ teaspoon dried cilantro leaves
½ teaspoon cumin seed
4 cups shredded leaf lettuce
2 avocados, peeled and cut into ½-inch cubes
1 medium tomato, seeded and chopped (about 1 cup)
1 can (8 oz.) corn, drained
2 tablespoons canned sliced jalapeño peppers, drained and chopped

4 servings

Prepare salad shells as directed on package. Set aside. In 1-cup measure, combine all dressing ingredients. Mix well. Set aside.

In 1-quart casserole, combine ground beef, lime juice, paprika, cilantro and cumin seed. Mix well. Microwave at High for 2 to 4 minutes, or until meat is no longer pink, stirring once to break apart. Drain. Set aside.

Place remaining ingredients in large mixing bowl. Toss to combine. Add dressing and ground beef mixture. Toss to combine. Spoon evenly into prepared salad shells. Garnish with red onion rings, if desired.

Per Serving:			
Calories:	633	Cholesterol:	35 mg.
Protein:	18 g.	Sodium:	467 mg.
Carbohydrate:	47 g.	Exchanges:	2 starch, 1 medium-fat meat,
Fat:	45 g.		3 vegetable, 8 fat

Chow Mein Salad

- 6 cups torn fresh spinach leaves
- 1 cup celery chunks (½-inch chunks)
- ½ cup julienne carrot (1½ × ¼-inch strips)
- 1 can (8 oz.) sliced water chestnuts, rinsed and drained
- 2 tablespoons sliced green onion
- 2 teaspoons cornstarch
- 1 teaspoon sugar
- ½ teaspoon ground ginger
- ¼ teaspoon garlic powder
- ⅔ cup chicken broth
- 3 tablespoons soy sauce
- ½ lb. lean ground beef, crumbled
- 2 cups chow mein noodles

4 servings

In large mixing bowl or salad bowl, combine spinach, celery, carrot and water chestnuts. Toss to combine. Set aside.

In 4-cup measure, combine onion, cornstarch, sugar, ginger and garlic powder. Mix well. Blend in broth and soy sauce. Mix well. Microwave at High for 3 to 4 minutes, or until dressing is thickened and translucent, stirring after first 2 minutes and then every minute. Set aside.

In 1-quart casserole, microwave ground beef at High for 2 to 4 minutes, or until meat is no longer pink, stirring once to break apart. Drain. Add dressing. Toss to coat. Add hot meat mixture to spinach mixture. Add chow mein noodles. Toss to coat. Serve immediately.

Per Serving:	
Calories:	311
Protein:	18 g.
Carbohydrate:	31 g.
Fat:	13 g.
Cholesterol:	38 mg.
Sodium:	1259 mg.
Exchanges:	1 starch, 1½ medium-fat meat, 3 vegetable, ½ fat

Pepper Beef & Pasta Salad

8 oz. uncooked rotini pasta
1 large green pepper, cut into 1-inch chunks (about 2 cups)
1 medium red pepper, cut into 1-inch chunks (about 1 cup)
1 medium yellow pepper, cut into 1-inch chunks (about 1 cup)
2 tablespoons water
⅓ cup sliced green onions
½ lb. lean ground beef, crumbled
⅓ cup teriyaki sauce
2 tablespoons vegetable oil
2 teaspoons sugar
½ teaspoon garlic powder
Leaf lettuce

4 servings

Prepare pasta as directed on package. Rinse and drain. Place in large mixing bowl or salad bowl. Set aside. In 2-quart casserole, combine peppers and water. Cover. Microwave at High for 3 to 5 minutes, or until tender-crisp, stirring once. Drain. Add peppers and green onions to pasta. Mix well. Set aside.

In 1-quart casserole, microwave ground beef at High for 2 to 4 minutes, or until no longer pink, stirring once to break apart. Drain. Set aside.

In 1-cup measure or small mixing bowl, combine remaining ingredients, except lettuce. Mix well. Add to beef. Stir to coat. Microwave at High for 1 to 2 minutes, or until hot, stirring once. Add to pasta mixture. Mix well. Serve salad immediately on lettuce-lined plates.

Per Serving:	
Calories:	428
Protein:	19 g.
Carbohydrate:	53 g.
Fat:	15 g.
Cholesterol:	35 mg.
Sodium:	553 mg.
Exchanges:	3 starch, 1 medium-fat meat, 1½ vegetable, 2 fat

Pizza Pasta Salad ▲

8 oz. uncooked rotelle pasta
1 cup sliced fresh mushrooms
1 cup green pepper strips (2 × ¼-inch)
1 cup shredded mozzarella cheese
2 oz. pepperoni slices, cut in half (about ½ cup)
½ lb. lean ground beef, crumbled
½ teaspoon Italian seasoning
1 can (8 oz.) pizza sauce

4 servings

Prepare pasta as directed on package. Rinse and drain. Place in large mixing bowl or salad bowl. Add mushrooms, pepper strips, cheese and pepperoni. Toss to combine. Set aside.

In 1-quart casserole, place ground beef and Italian seasoning. Mix well. Microwave at High for 2 to 4 minutes, or until meat is no longer pink, stirring once to break apart. Drain.

Add pizza sauce to ground beef. Microwave at High for 2 to 3 minutes, or until hot, stirring once. Add to pasta mixture. Toss to combine. Serve immediately.

Per Serving:			
Calories:	518	Cholesterol:	61 mg.
Protein:	29 g.	Sodium:	790 mg.
Carbohydrate:	53 g.	Exchanges:	3 starch, 2½ medium-fat meat, 1½ vegetable, 1½ fat
Fat:	20 g.		

Marinated Wild Rice & Beef Salad

- 1 cup uncooked long-grain wild rice (about 3 cups cooked)
- 3 cups frozen chopped broccoli
- 2 tablespoons water
- ½ lb. lean ground beef, crumbled
- 1 cup cherry tomatoes, cut in half
- ½ cup Italian dressing
- 1 jar (6 oz.) marinated artichoke hearts, undrained
- 1 jar (2 oz.) sliced pimiento, drained
- ¼ cup snipped fresh parsley Leaf lettuce
- ¼ cup sliced almonds

4 servings

Prepare wild rice as directed on package. Drain. Place hot cooked rice in large mixing bowl or salad bowl. Set aside.

In 2-quart casserole, combine broccoli and water. Cover. Microwave at High for 3 to 4 minutes, or until defrosted, stirring once to break apart. Drain. Add to rice. Set aside.

In 1-quart casserole, microwave ground beef at High for 2 to 4 minutes, or until meat is no longer pink, stirring once to break apart. Drain.

Add ground beef and remaining ingredients, except lettuce and almonds, to rice mixture. Toss to combine. Serve in lettuce-lined salad bowl. Sprinkle evenly with almonds. Serve immediately.

Per Serving:
Calories:	508
Protein:	21 g.
Carbohydrate:	45 g.
Fat:	29 g.
Cholesterol:	35 mg.
Sodium:	379 mg.
Exchanges:	2 starch, 1½ medium-fat meat, 3 vegetable, 4 fat

Hot German Beef & Bacon Salad

- 2 strips bacon, cut into ½-inch pieces
- 1 small red onion, cut in half and thinly sliced
- ½ cup chopped green pepper
- 1 cup frozen sliced carrots
- 2 tablespoons sugar
- 1 tablespoon all-purpose flour
- ¼ teaspoon freshly ground pepper
- ¼ teaspoon celery seed
- ½ cup water
- ¼ cup white vinegar
- 2 cans (16 oz. each) sliced potatoes, rinsed and drained
- ½ lb. lean ground beef, crumbled
- 2 cups torn fresh spinach leaves

4 servings

Place bacon in 2-quart casserole. Cover with paper towel. Microwave at High for 2 to 4 minutes, or until brown and crisp, stirring once. Add onion, green pepper and carrots. Mix well. Cover. Microwave at High for 4 to 6 minutes, or until vegetables are tender-crisp, stirring once.

Sprinkle vegetable mixture with sugar, flour, pepper and celery seed. Mix well. Blend in water and vinegar. Microwave at High, uncovered, for 4 to 6 minutes, or until mixture thickens and bubbles, stirring twice. Add potatoes. Mix well. Set aside.

In 1-quart casserole, microwave ground beef at High for 2 to 4 minutes, or until meat is no longer pink, stirring once to break apart. Drain. Add ground beef and spinach to potato mixture. Toss to combine. Microwave at High, uncovered, for 2 to 3 minutes, or just until mixture is hot and spinach begins to wilt, stirring once. Serve immediately.

Per Serving:
Calories:	273	Cholesterol:	38 mg.
Protein:	15 g.	Sodium:	491 mg.
Carbohydrate:	33 g.	Exchanges:	1½ starch, 1 medium-fat meat, 2 vegetable, 1 fat
Fat:	10 g.		

Tri-Bean & Beef Salad

1 can (15½ oz.) dark red
    kidney beans, rinsed and
    drained
1 can (15 oz.) garbanzo
    beans, rinsed and drained
1½ cups cherry tomatoes, cut in
    half
½ cup sliced green onions
¼ cup snipped fresh parsley
1 pkg. (9 oz.) frozen whole
    green beans
2 tablespoons water
½ lb. lean ground beef,
    crumbled
1 teaspoon dried thyme
    leaves
1 teaspoon Worcestershire
    sauce
½ cup white vinegar
¼ cup vegetable oil
1 teaspoon celery seed
1 teaspoon sugar
¼ teaspoon salt
¼ teaspoon pepper
    Leaf lettuce

4 servings

In large mixing bowl or salad bowl, combine kidney beans, garbanzo beans, tomatoes, onions and parsley. Set aside.

In 1-quart casserole, place green beans and water. Cover. Microwave at High for 4 to 6 minutes, or until defrosted, stirring once to break apart. Drain. Add to bean mixture. Set aside.

In 1-quart casserole, combine ground beef, thyme and Worcestershire sauce. Mix well. Microwave at High for 2 to 4 minutes, or until meat is no longer pink, stirring once to break apart. Drain. Add to bean mixture. Set aside.

In 1-cup measure, combine remaining ingredients, except lettuce. Mix well. Add to bean mixture. Toss to combine. Serve immediately on lettuce-lined plate.

Per Serving:			
Calories:	467	Cholesterol:	35 mg.
Protein:	23 g.	Sodium:	193 mg.
Carbohydrate:	44 g.	Exchanges:	2 starch, 1½ medium-fat meat,
Fat:	23 g.		3 vegetable, 2½ fat

Greek Vegetable & Beef Salad

Dressing:

⅓ cup olive oil
3 tablespoons red wine vinegar
1 tablespoon Dijon mustard
¼ teaspoon dried oregano
  leaves
⅛ teaspoon garlic powder

½ lb. lean ground beef,
  crumbled
1 teaspoon dried parsley flakes
¼ teaspoon dried oregano
  leaves
⅛ teaspoon garlic powder
4 cups torn romaine lettuce
1 medium cucumber, quartered
  lengthwise and sliced
  (about 2 cups)
1 medium tomato, seeded and
  chopped (about 1 cup)
1 cup crumbled feta cheese
  (about ¼ lb.)
½ cup coarsely chopped red
  onion
½ cup whole Kalamata olives or
  black olives

4 servings

In 1-cup measure, combine all dressing ingredients. Mix well. Set aside.

In 1-quart casserole, combine ground beef, parsley, oregano and garlic powder. Mix well. Microwave at High for 2 to 4 minutes, or until meat is no longer pink, stirring once to break apart. Drain. Set aside.

In large mixing bowl or salad bowl, combine lettuce, cucumber, tomato, cheese, onion and olives. Add dressing and ground beef. Toss to combine. Serve immediately.

Per Serving:		
Calories:	440	
Protein:	16 g.	
Carbohydrate:	9 g.	
Fat:	38 g.	
Cholesterol:	60 mg.	
Sodium:	1058 mg.	
Exchanges:	½ medium-fat meat, 2 vegetable, 6 fat	

Red Bean & Rice Salad

1 cup uncooked long-grain
  white rice (3 cups cooked)
1 can (15½ oz.) dark red kidney
  beans, rinsed and drained
1 medium green pepper, cut
  into ¾-inch chunks
1 cup cherry tomatoes,
  quartered
½ cup chopped onion
¼ cup snipped fresh parsley

½ lb. lean ground beef,
  crumbled
⅓ cup catsup
1 tablespoon vegetable oil
1 tablespoon red wine vinegar
½ teaspoon paprika
½ teaspoon ground cumin
¼ teaspoon ground cinnamon
¼ teaspoon cayenne

4 servings

Prepare rice as directed on package. In large mixing bowl or salad bowl, combine rice, beans, pepper, tomatoes, onion and parsley. Mix well. Set aside.

In 1-quart casserole, microwave ground beef at High for 2 to 4 minutes, or until meat is no longer pink, stirring once to break apart. Drain. Add to rice mixture. Set aside.

In small mixing bowl, combine remaining ingredients. Mix well. Add to rice mixture. Toss to coat. Serve immediately.

Per Serving:			
Calories:	441	Cholesterol:	35 mg.
Protein:	20 g.	Sodium:	275 mg.
Carbohydrate:	64 g.	Exchanges:	3½ starch, 1 medium-fat meat,
Fat:	12 g.		2 vegetable, 1 fat

Szechuan Salad

- 2 oz. uncooked cellophane noodles
- ½ cup vegetable oil
- ½ lb. lean ground beef, crumbled
- 4 cups shredded lettuce
- 1 cup grated carrots
- ½ cup sliced green onions
- ¼ cup hoisin sauce
- 2 tablespoons white wine vinegar
- 1 tablespoon plus 1 teaspoon soy sauce
- 1 teaspoon sesame oil
- 1 teaspoon sugar
- ¼ teaspoon crushed red pepper flakes
- ¼ cup finely chopped peanuts

4 to 6 servings

Break noodles into small pieces. Heat vegetable oil in Dutch oven conventionally over medium-high heat. Drop noodles by small handfuls into hot oil. Fry for 30 seconds to 1 minute, or until noodles are puffed, tossing gently several times. Drain on paper towels. Repeat with remaining noodles. Set aside.

In 1-quart casserole, microwave ground beef at High for 2 to 4 minutes, or until meat is no longer pink, stirring once to break apart. Drain. Set aside.

In large mixing bowl or salad bowl, combine lettuce, carrots and onions. Toss to combine. Set aside.

In 1-cup measure, combine remaining ingredients, except peanuts. Mix well. Add noodles, ground beef and hoisin sauce mixture to lettuce mixture. Toss to combine. Sprinkle with peanuts. Serve immediately.

Per Serving:	
Calories:	330
Protein:	9 g.
Carbohydrate:	15 g.
Fat:	27 g.
Cholesterol:	23 mg.
Sodium:	367 mg.
Exchanges:	½ starch, 1 medium-fat meat, 1½ vegetable, 4 fat

Cajun Rice Salad ▲

- 1 cup uncooked brown rice (3 cups cooked)
- 1 pkg. (10 oz.) frozen cut okra
- 1 cup frozen peas
- 2 tablespoons water
- ½ lb. lean ground beef, crumbled
- 1 teaspoon paprika
- ½ teaspoon cajun seasoning

Dressing:

- ¼ cup vegetable oil
- 2 tablespoons white wine vinegar
- 1 teaspoon cajun seasoning

- 1 cup seeded chopped tomato
- 1 can (8 oz.) corn, drained
- ¼ cup snipped fresh parsley

4 servings

Prepare rice as directed on package. Place rice in large mixing bowl or salad bowl. Set aside.

In 2-quart casserole, combine okra, peas and water. Cover. Microwave at High for 5 to 6 minutes, or until vegetables are defrosted, stirring once. Drain. Add to rice. Set aside.

In 1-quart casserole, combine ground beef, paprika and ½ teaspoon cajun seasoning. Mix well. Microwave at High for 2 to 4 minutes, or until meat is no longer pink, stirring once to break apart. Drain. Add to rice mixture. Set aside.

In 1-cup measure, combine all dressing ingredients. Mix well. Add dressing, tomato, corn and parsley to rice mixture. Toss to combine. Serve immediately.

Per Serving:			
Calories:	508	Cholesterol:	35 mg.
Protein:	19 g.	Sodium:	239 mg.
Carbohydrate:	60 g.	Exchanges:	3 starch, 1 medium-fat meat,
Fat:	23 g.		3 vegetable, 3½ fat

Sandwiches

Basic Hamburger

Basic Hamburgers

1 lb. lean ground beef, crumbled

One or more of the following:
1 tablespoon prepared horseradish
1 tablespoon finely chopped onion
1 tablespoon catsup
1 tablespoon barbecue sauce
1 teaspoon prepared mustard

1 teaspoon Worcestershire sauce
½ teaspoon seasoned salt
½ teaspoon chili powder
½ teaspoon celery salt
½ teaspoon Italian seasoning
¼ teaspoon garlic powder
¼ teaspoon onion powder
¼ teaspoon pepper

4 servings

Per Serving:			
Calories:	219	Cholesterol:	70 mg.
Protein:	20 g.	Sodium:	62 mg.
Carbohydrate:	—	Exchanges:	3 medium-fat meat
Fat:	15 g.		

Basic Stuffed Hamburgers ▶

1 lb. lean ground beef, crumbled
½ cup finely shredded cheese (Cheddar, Colby, Monterey Jack or mozzarella)

4 servings

Per Serving:	
Calories:	276
Protein:	23 g.
Carbohydrate:	—
Fat:	20 g.
Cholesterol:	85 mg.
Sodium:	150 mg.
Exchanges:	3 medium-fat meat, 1 fat

How to Microwave Basic Hamburgers

Combine ground beef and desired flavorings in medium mixing bowl. Divide mixture into 4 equal portions. Shape each portion into 4-inch round patty. Arrange on roasting rack.

Microwave at High for 4½ to 7½ minutes, or until meat is firm and no longer pink, turning once.

Let burgers stand, covered with wax paper, for 2 minutes before serving. Burgers may appear slightly pink on top center after microwaving (top); pink areas will disappear during standing time.

How to Microwave Basic Stuffed Hamburgers

Divide ground beef into 8 equal portions. Place each portion between sheets of plastic wrap, and press into 4-inch round patty. Place 2 tablespoons cheese in center of each of 4 patties.

Top with remaining patties. Press edges together to seal. Arrange on roasting rack. Microwave at High for 6 to 7 minutes, or until meat is firm and no longer pink, turning once.

Let burgers stand, covered with wax paper, for 2 minutes before serving. Burgers may appear slightly pink on top center after microwaving; pink areas will disappear during standing time.

Bacon-Cheese Stuffed Burgers

- 1 lb. lean ground beef, crumbled
- 1 egg
- 2 tablespoons unseasoned dry bread crumbs
- ¼ teaspoon garlic powder
- 2 strips bacon
- ½ cup shredded pasteurized process cheese loaf
- 2 tablespoons sliced green onion

4 servings

In medium mixing bowl, combine ground beef, egg, bread crumbs and garlic powder. Mix well. Set mixture aside.

Layer 3 paper towels on plate. Arrange bacon on paper towels. Cover with another paper towel. Microwave at High for 1½ to 2½ minutes, or until bacon is brown and crisp. Cool slightly. Crumble and place in small mixing bowl. Add cheese and onion. Toss to combine. Set aside.

Divide meat mixture into 8 equal portions. Shape each portion into 4-inch round patty. Divide cheese mixture into 4 portions. Place 1 portion in center of each of 4 patties. Top with remaining patties. Press edges together to seal. Arrange on roasting rack.

Microwave at High for 6 to 7 minutes, or until meat is firm and no longer pink, turning once.

Let burgers stand, covered with wax paper, for 2 minutes. Serve on hamburger buns with lettuce, tomato and onion, if desired.

Per Serving:
Calories:	326
Protein:	26 g.
Carbohydrate:	4 g.
Fat:	22 g.
Cholesterol:	152 mg.
Sodium:	408 mg.
Exchanges:	½ starch, 3½ medium-fat meat, 1 fat

Patty Melt on Rye ▲

- 2 medium onions, thinly sliced and separated into rings
- 2 tablespoons margarine or butter
- 1 lb. lean ground beef, crumbled
- 1 tablespoon Worcestershire sauce
- ½ teaspoon salt
- ¼ teaspoon pepper
- 4 slices (¾ oz. each) pasteurized process American cheese
- 8 slices rye bread, toasted

4 servings

In 2-quart casserole, combine onions and margarine. Cover. Microwave at High for 8 to 10 minutes, or until onions are tender, stirring twice. Set aside.

In medium mixing bowl, combine ground beef, Worcestershire sauce, salt and pepper. Mix well. Divide mixture into 4 equal portions. Shape each portion into 4-inch round patty. Arrange on roasting rack.

Microwave at High for 4½ to 7½ minutes, or until meat is firm and no longer pink, turning once. Top each patty evenly with onions. Top each with cheese slice.

Microwave at High for 1 to 2 minutes, or until cheese is melted. Place each patty melt between 2 toast slices.

Per Serving:
Calories:	489	Cholesterol:	91 mg.
Protein:	30 g.	Sodium:	1020 mg.
Carbohydrate:	30 g.	Exchanges:	2 starch, 3½ medium-fat meat, 2 fat
Fat:	28 g.		

Austrian Burgers

2 tablespoons Thousand Island dressing
¼ cup mayonnaise or salad dressing

Meat Mixture:
1 lb. lean ground beef, crumbled
1 egg
2 tablespoons stone-ground mustard
2 tablespoons unseasoned dry bread crumbs
¼ teaspoon salt

Filling:
1 can (8 oz.) sauerkraut, rinsed and drained, pressing to remove excess moisture, divided
½ cup finely shredded Swiss cheese
2 tablespoons finely chopped red pepper (optional)
¼ teaspoon caraway seed

4 onion or rye bagels, split and toasted
Leaf lettuce
Tomato slices
Onion slices

4 servings

In small bowl, combine dressing and mayonnaise. Mix well. Cover sauce with plastic wrap. Chill.

In medium mixing bowl, combine all meat mixture ingredients. Mix well. Set aside. In small mixing bowl, combine ½ cup sauerkraut and remaining filling ingredients. Set aside.

Divide meat mixture into 8 equal portions. Shape each portion into 4-inch round patty. Divide cheese mixture into 4 portions. Place 1 portion in center of each of 4 patties. Top with remaining patties. Press edges together to seal. Arrange on roasting rack.

Microwave at High for 6 to 7 minutes, or until meat is firm and no longer pink, turning once.

Let burgers stand, covered with wax paper, for 2 minutes. Spread insides of bagels evenly with sauce.

Arrange lettuce, tomato, onion slices, burgers and remaining sauerkraut evenly on bottom halves of bagels. Add bagel tops.

Per Serving:			
Calories:	614	Cholesterol:	162 mg.
Protein:	33 g.	Sodium:	975 mg.
Carbohydrate:	38 g.	Exchanges:	2 starch, 3½ medium-fat meat,
Fat:	36 g.		1½ vegetable, 3½ fat

Greek Burgers ▲

¼ cup sour cream
1 tablespoon milk
1 teaspoon dried dill weed, divided
1 cup seeded and finely chopped cucumber
¾ cup water
¼ cup uncooked bulgur or cracked wheat

1 lb. lean ground beef, crumbled
1 egg
2 teaspoons dried parsley flakes
¼ teaspoon garlic powder
¼ teaspoon salt
4 pitas (6-inch)
  Leaf lettuce
8 slices tomato

4 servings

In small mixing bowl, combine sour cream, milk and ½ teaspoon dill weed. Mix well. Add cucumber. Mix well. Cover with plastic wrap. Chill.

In 2-cup measure, microwave water at High for 2 to 3 minutes, or until boiling. Stir in bulgur. Cover with plastic wrap. Let stand about 30 minutes, or until bulgur softens. Drain, pressing to remove excess moisture.

Place bulgur in medium mixing bowl. Add ground beef, egg, parsley, remaining ½ teaspoon dill weed, the garlic powder and salt. Mix well. Divide mixture into 4 equal portions. Shape each portion into 4-inch round patty. Arrange on roasting rack. Microwave at High for 6 to 8 minutes, or until meat is firm and no longer pink, turning once. Let burgers stand, covered with wax paper, for 2 minutes.

Layer pitas between 2 dampened paper towels. Microwave at High for 1 to 2 minutes, or just until pitas are warm to the touch. Fold each pita in half. Place lettuce, 1 burger and 2 tomato slices in each pita. Spoon one-fourth of cucumber mixture into each pita. Secure with wooden pick.

Per Serving:			
Calories:	408	Cholesterol:	146 mg.
Protein:	27 g.	Sodium:	228 mg.
Carbohydrate:	28 g.	Exchanges:	1½ starch, 3 medium-fat meat,
Fat:	21 g.		1 vegetable, 1 fat

Italian Burgers

Meat Mixture:
1 lb. lean ground beef, crumbled
1 egg
¼ cup grated Parmesan cheese
1 tablespoon instant minced onion
½ teaspoon Italian seasoning
¼ teaspoon garlic powder

2 slices (1 oz. each) Provolone cheese, cut in half
4 French rolls (6-inch), split
  Leaf lettuce
4 tablespoons spaghetti sauce

4 servings

In medium mixing bowl, combine all meat mixture ingredients. Mix well. Divide mixture into 4 equal portions. Shape each portion into 5½ × 2½-inch oval patty. Arrange patties on roasting rack.

Microwave at High for 5 to 7 minutes, or until meat is firm and no longer pink, turning once.

Top each patty with cheese. Let burgers stand, covered with wax paper, for 2 minutes, or until cheese melts.

Line each French roll with lettuce. Place 1 burger in each roll and top with 1 tablespoon spaghetti sauce.

Per Serving:	
Calories:	539
Protein:	35 g.
Carbohydrate:	43 g.
Fat:	24 g.
Cholesterol:	156 mg.
Sodium:	833 mg.
Exchanges:	2 starch,
	3½ medium-fat meat,
	2½ vegetable, 1 fat

Brasserie Burgers

¼ cup sour cream
2 teaspoons Dijon mustard
8 slices French bread, 1 inch thick
¼ cup shredded fresh Parmesan cheese
8 oz. fresh mushrooms, sliced
2 tablespoons sherry
1 tablespoon margarine or butter
¼ teaspoon garlic powder

Meat Mixture:
1 lb. lean ground beef, crumbled
½ teaspoon bouquet garni seasoning
¼ teaspoon salt

Romaine lettuce leaves
8 whole green onions

4 servings

In small mixing bowl, combine sour cream and mustard. Mix well. Cover sauce with plastic wrap. Chill.

Arrange bread slices in even layer on large baking sheet. Place under conventional broiler 2 to 3 inches from heat. Broil until golden brown. Turn. Sprinkle evenly with Parmesan cheese. Broil until golden brown. Cover with foil to keep warm. Set aside.

In 1-quart casserole, combine mushrooms, sherry, margarine and garlic powder. Cover. Microwave at High for 4 to 6 minutes, or until mushrooms are tender, stirring once. Re-cover. Set aside.

In medium mixing bowl, combine all meat mixture ingredients. Mix well. Divide mixture into 4 equal portions. Shape each portion into 4-inch round patty. Arrange on roasting rack.

Microwave at High for 4½ to 7½ minutes, or until meat is firm and no longer pink, turning once. Let burgers stand, covered with wax paper, for 2 minutes.

Drain mushrooms. Place each burger on lettuce-lined toast slice. Top evenly with mushrooms and sauce. Top with remaining toast slice. Serve with onion.

Per Serving:			
Calories:	544	Cholesterol:	84 mg.
Protein:	31 g.	Sodium:	837 mg.
Carbohydrate:	45 g.	Exchanges:	2½ starch, 3 medium-fat meat,
Fat:	25 g.		1½ vegetable, 2 fat

Hot & Spicy Meatball Hoagies

Meatballs:

- 1 lb. lean ground beef, crumbled
- 1 egg
- ¼ cup grated Parmesan cheese
- 1 tablespoon instant minced onion

Sauce:

- 1 can (15 oz.) tomato sauce
- 1 teaspoon dried parsley flakes
- 1 teaspoon sugar
- ¼ teaspoon dried basil leaves
- ¼ teaspoon dried oregano leaves
- ¼ teaspoon crushed red pepper flakes
- ⅛ teaspoon garlic powder

- 4 hot dog buns, split
- 3 slices (¾ oz. each) Monterey Jack cheese, cut into quarters

4 servings

In medium mixing bowl, combine all meatball ingredients. Mix well. Shape into 16 meatballs, about 1½ inches in diameter. Arrange in single layer in 8-inch square baking dish. Microwave at High for 6 to 8 minutes, or until meatballs are firm and no longer pink, rearranging twice. Drain. Set aside.

In 2-quart casserole, combine all sauce ingredients. Mix well. Add meatballs to sauce. Stir to coat meatballs with sauce. Cover with wax paper. Microwave at High for 4 to 6 minutes, or until meatballs and sauce are hot, stirring once or twice.

Arrange 4 meatballs in each bun. Place on paper-towel-lined serving platter. Spoon sauce evenly over meatballs. Top each hoagie evenly with cheese. Microwave at High for 1 to 2 minutes, or until cheese is melted.

Per Serving:			
Calories:	484	Cholesterol:	160 mg.
Protein:	33 g.	Sodium:	1127 mg.
Carbohydrate:	31 g.	Exchanges:	1½ starch, 3½ medium-fat meat,
Fat:	25 g.		1½ vegetable, 1½ fat

Barbecue-topped Corn Muffins

- 1 medium onion, thinly sliced and separated into rings
- ½ cup thinly sliced celery
- ½ cup chopped green pepper
- 1 lb. lean ground beef, crumbled
- ¾ cup barbecue sauce
- ⅓ cup catsup
- 2 tablespoons packed brown sugar
- 1 tablespoon red wine vinegar
- 1 tablespoon prepared mustard
- ½ teaspoon liquid smoke flavoring
- ¼ teaspoon garlic powder
- ⅛ teaspoon red pepper sauce
- 6 corn muffins, quartered

6 servings

In 2-quart casserole, combine onion, celery and green pepper. Cover. Microwave at High for 4 to 5 minutes, or until vegetables are tender-crisp, stirring once. Add ground beef. Microwave at High, uncovered, for 4 to 7 minutes, or until meat is no longer pink, stirring twice to break meat apart. Set aside.

In small mixing bowl, combine remaining ingredients, except corn muffins. Mix well. Add to ground beef mixture. Mix well. Microwave at High for 4 to 5 minutes, or until mixture is hot and flavors are blended. Spoon evenly over corn muffins.

Per Serving:
Calories:	308
Protein:	17 g.
Carbohydrate:	28 g.
Fat:	14 g.
Cholesterol:	74 mg.
Sodium:	795 mg.
Exchanges:	1½ starch, 1½ medium-fat meat, 1 vegetable, 1½ fat

Stuffed Pizza Sandwiches

- 1 loaf (1 lb.) French bread
- 1 lb. lean ground beef, crumbled
- 1 cup chopped green pepper
- 1 teaspoon Italian seasoning
- 1 can (8 oz.) pizza sauce
- 1½ cups shredded mozzarella cheese

8 servings

Trim ends from French bread. Cut loaf in half vertically. Using long, serrated knife, remove bread from center of each loaf half, leaving ¼-inch shell. Reserve bread for future use. Set halves aside.

In 2-quart casserole, combine ground beef, pepper and Italian seasoning. Microwave at High for 4 to 7 minutes, or until meat is no longer pink, stirring twice to break apart. Drain. Add pizza sauce and cheese. Mix well. Divide mixture in half.

Stuff each loaf half with half of filling mixture. Place filled loaf halves on roasting rack. Cover with wax paper. Microwave at 50% (Medium) for 3 to 4 minutes, or just until warm to the touch, rearranging once. To serve, slice each loaf half into four 1½-inch slices.

Per Serving:
Calories:	356
Protein:	21 g.
Carbohydrate:	36 g.
Fat:	13 g.
Cholesterol:	48 mg.
Sodium:	631 mg.
Exchanges:	2 starch,
	2 medium-fat meat,
	1 vegetable, ½ fat

Open-face Vegetable-Beef Sandwich

1½ cups sliced fresh
    mushrooms
 1 cup thinly sliced zucchini
 1 cup thinly sliced yellow
    summer squash
 1 medium onion, thinly sliced
    and separated into rings
 1 tablespoon Worcestershire
    sauce
¼ teaspoon salt
⅛ teaspoon pepper
 1 cup seeded chopped
    tomato
½ lb. lean ground beef,
    crumbled
 1 teaspoon dried parsley
    flakes
½ teaspoon dried basil leaves
 6 slices sourdough bread,
    toasted
¾ cup shredded Monterey
    Jack cheese

6 servings

In 2-quart casserole, combine mushrooms, zucchini, squash, onion, Worcestershire sauce, salt and pepper. Mix well. Cover. Microwave at High for 6 to 8 minutes, or until vegetables are tender, stirring once. Drain. Add tomato. Mix well. Set aside.

In 1-quart casserole, combine ground beef, parsley and basil. Mix well. Microwave at High for 2 to 4 minutes, or until meat is no longer pink, stirring once to break apart. Drain. Add to vegetable mixture. Mix well.

Top each toast slice with ½ cup meat mixture. Sprinkle each with 2 tablespoons cheese. Arrange 3 sandwiches on paper-towel-lined serving platter.

Microwave at High for 45 seconds to 1 minute, or until cheese is melted. Repeat with remaining sandwiches.

Per Serving:			
Calories:	252	Cholesterol:	37 mg.
Protein:	15 g.	Sodium:	421 mg.
Carbohydrate:	25 g.	Exchanges:	1 starch, 1 medium-fat meat,
Fat:	11 g.		2 vegetable, 1 fat

Chilies, Soups & Stews

Black Bean & Beef Chili

Chilies

Cincinnati Chili

1 lb. lean ground beef, crumbled
1 can (16 oz.) whole tomatoes, undrained and cut up
1 can (8 oz.) tomato sauce
1 tablespoon chili powder
¼ teaspoon ground cumin
¼ teaspoon garlic powder
¼ teaspoon dried oregano leaves
¼ teaspoon salt
⅛ teaspoon ground cinnamon
Hot cooked spaghetti

6 servings

In 2-quart casserole, microwave ground beef at High for 4 to 7 minutes, or just until meat loses pink color, stirring twice to break apart.

Add remaining ingredients, except spaghetti. Mix well. Cover with wax paper. Microwave at High for 8 to 10 minutes, or until flavors are blended and chili is hot, stirring once or twice. Serve chili over spaghetti.

Variation 1: Follow recipe above, except add 1 can (15½ oz.) kidney beans, rinsed and drained, when adding remaining ingredients.

◄ **Variation 2:** Follow Variation 1, above. Serve chili topped with finely shredded Cheddar cheese and finely chopped onion.

Per Serving:	
Calories:	275
Protein:	18 g.
Carbohydrate:	27 g.
Fat:	11 g.
Cholesterol:	47 mg.
Sodium:	534 mg.
Exchanges:	1 starch, 1½ medium-fat meat, 2½ vegetable, ½ fat

White Bean Chili

½ cup sliced celery
½ medium green pepper, cut into ½-inch chunks
½ cup chopped onion
¼ cup water
½ lb. lean ground beef, crumbled
1 can (19 oz.) white kidney beans, rinsed and drained
1 can (14½ oz.) diced tomatoes, undrained
1 can (8 oz.) tomato sauce
2 teaspoons chili powder
½ teaspoon ground cumin

6 servings

In 2-quart casserole, combine celery, pepper, onion and water. Cover. Microwave at High for 5 to 6 minutes, or until vegetables are tender, stirring once.

Add ground beef. Microwave at High, uncovered, for 2 to 4 minutes, or just until meat loses pink color, stirring once to break apart.

Add remaining ingredients. Mix well. Cover with wax paper. Microwave at High for 8 to 14 minutes, or until flavors are blended and chili is hot, stirring once or twice.

Per Serving:	
Calories:	180
Protein:	13 g.
Carbohydrate:	21 g.
Fat:	6 g.
Cholesterol:	23 mg.
Sodium:	381 mg.
Exchanges:	1 starch, 1 medium-fat meat, 1½ vegetable

Quick & Easy Chili

½ cup thinly sliced celery
3 tablespoons instant minced onion
1 tablespoon vegetable oil
¼ teaspoon instant minced garlic
1 lb. lean ground beef, crumbled
1 can (16 oz.) kidney beans, rinsed and drained
1 can (14½ oz.) diced tomatoes, undrained
1 can (8 oz.) tomato sauce
1 tablespoon chili powder
½ teaspoon salt

6 servings

In 2-quart casserole, combine celery, onion, oil and garlic. Cover. Microwave at High for 3 to 4 minutes, or until celery is tender, stirring once.

Add ground beef. Microwave at High, uncovered, for 4 to 7 minutes, or just until meat loses pink color, stirring twice to break apart.

Add remaining ingredients. Mix well. Cover with wax paper. Microwave at High for 10 to 15 minutes, or until flavors are blended and chili is hot, stirring once or twice.

Per Serving:	
Calories:	262
Protein:	19 g.
Carbohydrate:	19 g.
Fat:	13 g.
Cholesterol:	47 mg.
Sodium:	582 mg.
Exchanges:	1 starch, 2 medium-fat meat, 1 vegetable, ½ fat

Black Bean & Beef Chili

½ medium green pepper, cut into ½-inch chunks
½ cup chopped onion
2 tablespoons water
½ teaspoon instant minced garlic
½ lb. lean ground beef, crumbled
2 cans (15 oz. each) black beans, rinsed and drained
1 can (15 oz.) tomato sauce
1 can (14½ oz.) diced tomatoes, undrained
2 teaspoons chili powder
1 teaspoon paprika
½ teaspoon ground cumin
½ teaspoon dried oregano leaves
¼ teaspoon cayenne
1 bay leaf

6 servings

In 2-quart casserole, combine pepper, onion, water and garlic. Cover. Microwave at High for 3 to 4 minutes, or until vegetables are tender, stirring once.

Add ground beef. Microwave at High, uncovered, for 2 to 4 minutes, or just until meat loses pink color, stirring once to break apart.

Add remaining ingredients. Mix well. Cover with wax paper. Microwave at High for 20 to 30 minutes, or until flavors are blended and chili is hot, stirring once or twice. Remove and discard bay leaf.

Per Serving:			
Calories:	238	Cholesterol:	23 mg.
Protein:	16 g.	Sodium:	468 mg.
Carbohydrate:	32 g.	Exchanges:	1 starch, 1 medium-fat meat,
Fat:	6 g.		3 vegetable

Cornmeal-topped Chili con Carne*

Chili:

- 1 cup green pepper strips (2 × ¼-inch)
- ½ cup chopped onion
- 2 tablespoons water
- 1 lb. lean ground beef, crumbled
- 1 can (15 oz.) tomato purée
- 1 can (14½ oz.) diced tomatoes, drained
- 2 teaspoons chili powder
- ¼ teaspoon cumin seed
- ¼ teaspoon garlic powder
- ¼ teaspoon salt

Topping:

- 1 cup buttermilk baking mix
- ⅔ cup yellow cornmeal
- ½ cup milk
- 1 egg, slightly beaten

6 servings

*Recipe not recommended for ovens with less than 600 cooking watts.

Per Serving:	
Calories:	353
Protein:	20 g.
Carbohydrate:	36 g.
Fat:	15 g.
Cholesterol:	94 mg.
Sodium:	683 mg.
Exchanges:	1½ starch, 1½ medium-fat meat, 3 vegetable, 1½ fat

How to Microwave Cornmeal-topped Chili con Carne

Place pepper, onion and water in 2-quart casserole. Cover. Microwave at High for 5 to 8 minutes, or until vegetables are tender, stirring once. Drain.

Add remaining chili ingredients. Mix well. Cover with wax paper. Microwave at High for 8 to 12 minutes, or until meat is no longer pink and chili is hot, stirring twice to break apart. Set aside.

Combine topping ingredients in medium mixing bowl. Blend just until moistened. Divide mixture into six portions. Drop by spoonfuls onto top of chili mixture.

Microwave at High for 7 to 8 minutes, or until topping is light and springy to the touch, rotating casserole 2 or 3 times.

Southwestern Chili

½ cup chopped onion
1 tablespoon vegetable oil
¼ teaspoon ground cumin
¼ teaspoon dried oregano leaves
¼ teaspoon instant minced garlic
½ lb. lean ground beef, crumbled
1 can (16 oz.) diced tomatoes, undrained
1 can (16 oz.) pinto beans, rinsed and drained
1 can (12 oz.) corn with red and green peppers, drained
1 can (8 oz.) tomato sauce
1 can (4 oz.) chopped green chilies, drained
2 tablespoons canned sliced jalapeño peppers (optional)
1 tablespoon chili powder
1 teaspoon sugar

6 servings

In 2-quart casserole, combine onion, oil, cumin, oregano and garlic. Cover. Microwave at High for 3 to 4 minutes, or until onion is tender, stirring once.

Add ground beef. Microwave at High, uncovered, for 2 to 4 minutes, or just until meat loses pink color, stirring once to break apart.

Add remaining ingredients. Mix well. Cover with wax paper. Microwave at High for 10 to 15 minutes, or until flavors are blended and chili is hot, stirring once or twice.

Per Serving:
Calories:	239
Protein:	13 g.
Carbohydrate:	31 g.
Fat:	8 g.
Cholesterol:	23 mg.
Sodium:	548 mg.
Exchanges:	1½ starch, 1 medium-fat meat, 1½ vegetable, ½ fat

Vegetable-Beef Chili

- 1 medium zucchini (about 8 oz.), thinly sliced
- ½ cup chopped green pepper
- ½ cup chopped onion
- ¼ cup water
- ½ lb. lean ground beef, crumbled
- 2 cups frozen sliced carrots
- 1 can (15½ oz.) kidney beans, rinsed and drained
- 1 can (15 oz.) garbanzo beans, rinsed and drained
- 1 can (15 oz.) tomato sauce
- 1 tablespoon chili powder
- 1 teaspoon sugar
- ½ teaspoon salt
- ½ teaspoon ground cumin
- ½ teaspoon dried oregano leaves

6 to 8 servings

In 3-quart casserole, combine zucchini, pepper, onion and water. Cover. Microwave at High for 6 to 8 minutes, or until vegetables are tender, stirring once.

Add ground beef. Microwave at High, uncovered, for 2 to 4 minutes, or just until meat loses pink color, stirring once to break apart.

Add remaining ingredients. Mix well. Cover with wax paper. Microwave at High for 25 to 30 minutes, or until flavors are blended and chili is hot, stirring twice.

Per Serving:
Calories:	195
Protein:	12 g.
Carbohydrate:	27 g.
Fat:	5 g.
Cholesterol:	18 mg.
Sodium:	495 mg.
Exchanges:	1 starch, ½ medium-fat meat, 2 vegetable, ½ fat

Soups

◄ Chunky Tomato Soup

½ cup chopped green pepper
½ cup plus 1 tablespoon water, divided
½ lb. lean ground beef, crumbled
1 can (14½ oz.) diced tomatoes, undrained
1 can (10¾ oz.) condensed tomato soup
1 teaspoon sugar
½ teaspoon dried basil leaves

4 servings

In 2-quart casserole, combine pepper and 1 tablespoon water. Cover. Microwave at High for 2 to 4 minutes, or until pepper is tender, stirring once.

Add ground beef. Microwave at High, uncovered, for 2 to 4 minutes, or just until meat loses pink color, stirring once to break apart. Add remaining ½ cup water and remaining ingredients. Mix well. Cover. Microwave at High for 5 to 7 minutes, or until soup is hot, stirring once.

Per Serving:			
Calories:	191	Cholesterol:	35 mg.
Protein:	12 g.	Sodium:	729 mg.
Carbohydrate:	17 g.	Exchanges:	½ starch, 1 medium-fat meat,
Fat:	9 g.		2 vegetable, ½ fat

Hot & Sour Beef Soup

½ lb. lean ground beef, crumbled
2 teaspoons instant minced onion
¼ teaspoon ground ginger
¼ teaspoon instant minced garlic
2 tablespoons cornstarch
2 teaspoons sugar
½ teaspoon crushed red pepper flakes
2 cans (14½ oz. each) ready-to-serve chicken broth (3½ cups)
1 pkg. (16 oz.) frozen broccoli, cauliflower and carrots
½ cup water
1 tablespoon chili sauce
1 tablespoon soy sauce
1 tablespoon white vinegar

6 servings

In medium mixing bowl, combine ground beef, onion, ginger and garlic. Mix well. Shape into 30 meatballs, about ½ inch in diameter. Arrange meatballs in single layer in 8-inch square baking dish. Microwave at High for 3 to 4 minutes, or until meatballs are firm and no longer pink, rearranging once. Drain. Set aside.

In 3-quart casserole, combine cornstarch, sugar and red pepper flakes. Blend in chicken broth. Add remaining ingredients. Cover. Microwave at High for 20 to 25 minutes, or until mixture is slightly thickened and translucent, stirring twice.

Add meatballs. Re-cover. Microwave at High for 3 to 4 minutes, or until soup is hot, stirring once.

Per Serving:			
Calories:	147	Cholesterol:	23 mg.
Protein:	11 g.	Sodium:	687 mg.
Carbohydrate:	13 g.	Exchanges:	1 medium-fat meat, 2½ vegetable
Fat:	6 g.		

Meatball Carbonade

½ lb. lean ground beef, crumbled
½ teaspoon instant minced garlic
1 medium onion, sliced and separated into rings
2 slices bacon, cut into 1-inch pieces
¼ cup all-purpose flour
¼ teaspoon dried thyme leaves
¼ teaspoon salt
¼ teaspoon pepper
1 can (14½ oz.) ready-to-serve beef broth (1¾ cups)
1 can (12 oz.) beer
2 tablespoons tomato paste
1 can (16 oz.) sliced potatoes, drained
1 cup frozen sliced carrots
2 tablespoons dried parsley flakes
1 bay leaf

4 to 6 servings

In medium mixing bowl, combine ground beef and garlic. Shape into 24 meatballs, about ¾ inch in diameter. Set aside.

In 2-quart casserole, combine onion and bacon. Cover. Microwave at High for 5 to 6 minutes, or until onion is tender, stirring once or twice.

Stir in flour, thyme, salt and pepper. Blend in broth, beer and tomato paste. Add remaining ingredients. Mix well. Microwave at High, uncovered, for 10 minutes, stirring 2 or 3 times.

Add meatballs. Microwave at High for 10 to 12 minutes, or until meatballs are firm and no longer pink, stirring twice. Remove and discard bay leaf.

Per Serving:
Calories: 182
Protein: 10 g.
Carbohydrate: 17 g.
Fat: 6 g.
Cholesterol: 25 mg.
Sodium: 552 mg.
Exchanges: 1 starch, 1 medium-fat meat, ½ vegetable

Swedish Meatball Chowder

3¼ cups milk, divided
½ cup soft bread crumbs
½ lb. lean ground beef, crumbled
¼ cup plus 2 tablespoons snipped fresh parsley, divided
1 egg, slightly beaten
1 tablespoon instant minced onion
½ teaspoon ground nutmeg, divided
¼ teaspoon salt
¼ teaspoon ground ginger
¼ cup plus 2 tablespoons all-purpose flour
1 teaspoon instant beef bouillon granules
¼ teaspoon pepper
1 cup frozen sliced carrots
1 cup frozen peas

4 to 6 servings

In medium mixing bowl, combine ¼ cup milk and the bread crumbs. Let soak for 10 minutes. Add ground beef, ¼ cup parsley, the egg, onion, ¼ teaspoon nutmeg, the salt and ginger. Mix well.

Shape into 24 meatballs, about ¾ inch in diameter. Arrange meatballs in single layer in 8-inch square baking dish. Microwave at High for 4 to 6 minutes, or until meatballs are firm and no longer pink, rearranging once. Drain. Set aside.

In 2-quart casserole, combine remaining 2 tablespoons parsley, ¼ teaspoon nutmeg, the flour, bouillon granules and pepper. Mix well. Blend in remaining 3 cups milk. Mix well. Microwave at High, uncovered, for 10 to 12 minutes, or until mixture is thickened, stirring 3 times.

Add meatballs, carrots and peas. Microwave at High for 5 to 7 minutes, or until soup is hot, stirring twice.

Per Serving:			
Calories:	223	Cholesterol:	79 mg.
Protein:	15 g.	Sodium:	299 mg.
Carbohydrate:	21 g.	Exchanges:	½ starch, 1 medium-fat meat,
Fat:	9 g.		1½ vegetable, ½ low-fat milk

Borscht with Meatballs

½ lb. lean ground beef,
   crumbled
½ teaspoon dried dill weed,
   divided
⅛ teaspoon pepper
1 medium onion, thinly sliced
   and separated into rings
2 tablespoons margarine or
   butter
¼ teaspoon instant minced
   garlic
2 cans (14½ oz. each) ready-
   to-serve beef broth
   (3½ cups)
1 can (16 oz.) julienne beets,
   undrained
2 cups finely shredded red
   cabbage
2 tablespoons red wine vinegar
1 tablespoon packed brown
   sugar
¼ teaspoon salt
½ cup sour cream

8 servings

In medium mixing bowl, combine ground beef, ¼ teaspoon dill weed and the pepper. Mix well. Shape into 24 meatballs, about ¾ inch in diameter. Set aside.

In 3-quart casserole, combine onion, margarine and garlic. Cover. Microwave at High for 4 to 5 minutes, or until onion is tender, stirring once. Add broth, beets, cabbage, vinegar, brown sugar and salt to onion mixture. Mix well. Re-cover. Microwave at High for 10 minutes.

Add meatballs. Mix well. Re-cover. Microwave at High for 4 to 7 minutes, or until meatballs are firm and no longer pink, stirring once. In small bowl, combine remaining ¼ teaspoon dill weed and the sour cream. Mix well. Top each serving with 1 tablespoon of sour cream mixture.

Per Serving:			
Calories:	152	Cholesterol:	24 mg.
Protein:	8 g.	Sodium:	611 mg.
Carbohydrate:	8 g.	Exchanges:	½ medium-fat meat, 1½ vegetable,
Fat:	10 g.		1½ fat

Greek Meatball Soup

½ lb. lean ground beef, crumbled
½ teaspoon dried mint leaves
¼ teaspoon instant minced garlic
2 cans (14½ oz. each) ready-to-serve chicken broth (3½ cups)
1 cup uncooked instant white rice
¼ teaspoon salt
2 eggs, well beaten
3 tablespoons lemon juice
⅓ cup diagonally sliced green onions

4 to 6 servings

In medium mixing bowl, combine ground beef, mint leaves and garlic. Mix well. Shape into 24 meatballs, about ¾ inch in diameter.

Arrange meatballs in single layer in 8-inch square baking dish. Microwave at High for 3 to 4 minutes, or until meatballs are firm and no longer pink, rearranging once. Drain. Set aside.

In 2-quart casserole, combine broth, rice and salt. Cover. Microwave at High for 10 to 15 minutes, or until rice is tender, stirring once.

In 1-cup measure, combine eggs and lemon juice. Pour egg mixture in thin stream into soup, stirring constantly. Add meatballs. Re-cover. Let stand for 3 minutes. Sprinkle each serving evenly with green onions.

Per Serving:	
Calories:	142
Protein:	12 g.
Carbohydrate:	6 g.
Fat:	8 g.
Cholesterol:	115 mg.
Sodium:	569 mg.
Exchanges:	½ starch, 1½ medium-fat meat

Hamburger Barley Soup ▲

1 cup thinly sliced carrot
½ cup sliced celery
½ cup chopped green pepper
½ cup chopped onion
1¾ cups water, divided
½ lb. lean ground beef, crumbled
1 can (16 oz.) whole tomatoes, undrained and cut up
1 can (8 oz.) tomato sauce
⅓ cup quick-cooking barley
1 teaspoon instant beef bouillon granules
¼ teaspoon pepper
1 bay leaf

4 to 6 servings

In 3-quart casserole, combine carrot, celery, green pepper, onion and ¼ cup water. Cover. Microwave at High for 5 to 8 minutes, or until vegetables are tender, stirring once.

Add ground beef. Microwave at High, uncovered, for 2 to 4 minutes, or just until meat loses pink color, stirring once to break apart.

Add remaining 1½ cups water and remaining ingredients. Mix well. Cover. Microwave at High for 25 to 35 minutes, or until barley is tender, stirring 2 or 3 times. Remove and discard bay leaf.

Per Serving:			
Calories:	144	Cholesterol:	23 mg.
Protein:	9 g.	Sodium:	449 mg.
Carbohydrate:	15 g.	Exchanges:	1 starch, 1 medium-fat meat
Fat:	6 g.		

◀ Wonton Soup

Filling:

½ lb. lean ground beef, crumbled
¼ cup sliced green onions
1 tablespoon soy sauce
1 teaspoon cornstarch
½ teaspoon sugar
¼ teaspoon ground ginger
¼ teaspoon sesame oil
¼ teaspoon white pepper

18 wonton skins (3½-inch square)

1 egg yolk, slightly beaten
3 cans (14½ oz. each) ready-to-serve chicken broth (5¼ cups)
4 oz. fresh snow pea pods, sliced lengthwise into thin strips (about 1 cup)
1 cup sliced fresh mushrooms
¼ cup sliced green onions
1 teaspoon soy sauce
¼ teaspoon sesame oil

6 servings

Per Serving:	
Calories:	187
Protein:	14 g.
Carbohydrate:	11 g.
Fat:	9 g.
Cholesterol:	69 mg.
Sodium:	1057 mg.
Exchanges:	½ starch, 1 medium-fat meat, 1 vegetable, 1 fat

How to Microwave Wonton Soup

Combine all filling ingredients in medium mixing bowl. Mix well. Spoon 2 teaspoons of filling onto center of each wonton skin.

Brush edges of wonton skins lightly with egg yolk. Fold bottom corner over filling to opposite corner, forming triangle; press lightly to seal. Bring long corners together, pressing to seal. Cover wontons with damp towel. Set aside.

Combine remaining ingredients in 3-quart casserole. Cover. Microwave at High for 10 minutes. Add wontons. Re-cover. Microwave at High for 10 to 15 minutes, or until wonton filling is firm and wonton skins are tender, stirring twice.

Potato Chowder

½ lb. lean ground beef, crumbled
½ lb. new potatoes, cut into ½-inch chunks (about 2 cups)
½ cup chopped onion
¼ cup water
2 cups frozen mixed vegetables
1½ cups milk
1 can (10¾ oz.) condensed cream of mushroom soup
¼ teaspoon pepper
¼ teaspoon dried thyme leaves

6 servings

Layer 4 paper towels in 1-quart casserole. Place ground beef in casserole. Microwave at High for 2 to 4 minutes, or just until meat loses pink color, stirring once to break apart. Lift one side of paper towels, allowing ground beef to fall into casserole. Discard paper towels. Set ground beef aside.

In 2-quart casserole, combine potatoes, onion and water. Cover. Microwave at High for 7 to 10 minutes, or until potatoes are tender, stirring once. Add cooked ground beef and remaining ingredients. Mix well. Re-cover. Microwave at High for 8 to 12 minutes, or until chowder is hot, stirring twice.

Per Serving:				
Calories:	239	Cholesterol:	28 mg.
Protein:	12 g.	Sodium:	489 mg.
Carbohydrate:	24 g.	Exchanges:	1 starch, 1 medium-fat meat, 2 vegetable, 1 fat
Fat:	10 g.		

Cheesy Swiss Beef Soup ▲

½ lb. lean ground beef, crumbled
2 tablespoons margarine or butter
2 tablespoons all-purpose flour
  Dash white pepper
2½ cups milk

4 slices (¾ oz. each) processed Swiss cheese, torn into small pieces
1½ cups frozen mixed vegetables
¾ cup seeded chopped tomato

4 servings

In 1-quart casserole, microwave ground beef at High for 2 to 4 minutes, or just until meat loses pink color, stirring once to break apart. Drain. Set aside. In 2-quart casserole, microwave margarine at High for 45 seconds to 1 minute, or until melted. Stir in flour and pepper. Blend in milk. Microwave at High for 7 to 10 minutes, or until mixture thickens and bubbles, stirring 3 times.

Stir in cheese until melted. Add cooked ground beef, mixed vegetables and tomato. Mix well. Microwave at 70% (Medium High) for 5 to 8 minutes, or until soup is hot, stirring 2 or 3 times.

Per Serving:			
Calories:	367	Cholesterol:	64 mg.
Protein:	22 g.	Sodium:	535 mg.
Carbohydrate:	22 g.	Exchanges:	½ starch, 1 medium-fat meat,
Fat:	21 g.		1 high-fat meat, 1½ vegetable,
			½ low-fat milk, 1 fat

Cabbage Soup

2 cups finely shredded cabbage
½ cup chopped onion
½ cup water
¼ teaspoon instant minced garlic
½ lb. lean ground beef, crumbled
1 can (28 oz.) whole tomatoes, undrained and cut up
1 can (14½ oz.) ready-to-serve beef broth (1¾ cups)
1 can (6 oz.) tomato paste
½ cup uncooked instant rice
1 tablespoon packed brown sugar
½ teaspoon Worcestershire sauce
¼ teaspoon ground allspice

4 to 6 servings

In 3-quart casserole, combine cabbage, onion, water and garlic. Cover. Microwave at High for 5 to 8 minutes, or until cabbage is tender-crisp, stirring once.

Add ground beef. Microwave at High, uncovered, for 2 to 4 minutes, or just until meat loses pink color, stirring once to break apart.

Add remaining ingredients. Mix well. Cover. Microwave at High for 20 to 25 minutes, or until rice is tender, stirring twice.

Per Serving:	
Calories:	156
Protein:	10 g.
Carbohydrate:	18 g.
Fat:	6 g.
Cholesterol:	23 mg.
Sodium:	693 mg.
Exchanges:	½ starch,
	1 medium-fat meat,
	2 vegetable

Alphabet Beef Soup ▶

½ cup chopped celery
1 small onion, thinly sliced and separated into rings
2 tablespoons water
½ lb. lean ground beef, crumbled
2 cans (14½ oz. each) ready-to-serve beef broth (3½ cups)
2 cups water
1 can (15½ oz.) diced rutabagas, drained
1½ cups frozen sliced carrots
½ cup uncooked alphabet pasta
¼ cup snipped fresh parsley
1 teaspoon Worcestershire sauce
½ teaspoon salt
⅛ teaspoon pepper
1 bay leaf

6 servings

In 3-quart casserole, combine celery, onion and water. Cover. Microwave at High for 5 to 6 minutes, or until vegetables are tender, stirring once.

Add ground beef. Microwave at High, uncovered, for 2 to 4 minutes, or just until meat loses pink color, stirring once to break apart.

Add remaining ingredients. Cover. Microwave at High for 20 to 25 minutes, or until pasta is tender, stirring twice. Remove and discard bay leaf.

Per Serving:
Calories: 130
Protein: 10 g.
Carbohydrate: 10 g.
Fat: 6 g.
Cholesterol: 26 mg.
Sodium: 683 mg.
Exchanges: 1 medium-fat meat, 2 vegetable

Minestrone Soup

½ cup chopped onion
1 tablespoon vegetable oil
½ lb. lean ground beef, crumbled
2 cans (14½ oz. each) ready-to-serve beef broth (3½ cups)
2 cups frozen mixed vegetables
1 can (15 oz.) kidney beans, rinsed and drained
1 can (14½ oz.) diced tomatoes, undrained
1 cup uncooked medium macaroni shells
½ teaspoon celery salt
½ teaspoon Italian seasoning
1 bay leaf

8 servings

In 3-quart casserole, combine onion and oil. Cover. Microwave at High for 3 to 4 minutes, or until onion is tender, stirring once.

Add ground beef. Microwave at High, uncovered, for 2 to 4 minutes, or just until meat loses pink color, stirring once to break apart.

Add remaining ingredients. Mix well. Cover. Microwave at High for 25 to 35 minutes, or until macaroni is tender, stirring 2 or 3 times. Remove and discard bay leaf.

Per Serving:
Calories: 197
Protein: 12 g.
Carbohydrate: 23 g.
Fat: 6 g.
Cholesterol: 18 mg.
Sodium: 562 mg.
Exchanges: 1 starch, 1 medium-fat meat, 1½ vegetable

Beef & Tortellini Soup ▲

½ lb. lean ground beef,
    crumbled
1 teaspoon Italian seasoning
⅛ teaspoon garlic powder
1 can (28 oz.) whole tomatoes,
    undrained and cut up
1 pkg. (16 oz.) frozen
    cauliflower, zucchini, carrots
    and red pepper

1 can (14½ oz.) ready-to-serve
    beef broth (1¾ cups)
4 oz. fresh uncooked cheese-
    filled tortellini (about 1 cup)
¼ cup red wine
¼ teaspoon salt

6 to 8 servings

In 3-quart casserole, combine ground beef, Italian seasoning and garlic powder. Mix well. Microwave at High for 2 to 4 minutes, or just until
meat loses pink color, stirring once to break apart.

Add remaining ingredients. Mix well. Cover. Microwave at High for 25
to 30 minutes, or until tortellini is tender, stirring twice.

Per Serving:				
Calories:	150	Cholesterol:	25 mg.	
Protein:	10 g.	Sodium:	493 mg.	
Carbohydrate:	17 g.	Exchanges:	½ starch, ½ medium-fat meat,	
Fat:	5 g.		2 vegetable, ½ fat	

Wild Rice Soup

½ cup uncooked wild rice
    (about 1 cup, cooked)
½ cup sliced celery
½ cup chopped onion
1 tablespoon margarine or
    butter
½ lb. lean ground beef,
    crumbled
⅓ cup all-purpose flour
2 cans (14½ oz. each) ready-to-
    serve beef broth (3½ cups)
1 cup frozen sliced carrots,
    chopped
1 can (4 oz.) mushroom pieces
    and stems, drained

4 to 6 servings

Prepare wild rice as directed on
package. Drain. Set aside. In 2-
quart casserole, combine celery,
onion and margarine. Cover.
Microwave at High for 3 to 4
minutes, or until vegetables are
tender, stirring once.

Add ground beef. Microwave at
High, uncovered, for 2 to 4 minutes, or just until meat loses pink
color, stirring once to break apart.

Stir in flour. Blend in broth. Add
cooked wild rice, the carrots
and mushrooms. Mix well. Cover.
Microwave at High for 10 to 12
minutes, or until soup thickens
and bubbles, stirring twice.

Per Serving:	
Calories:	191
Protein:	12 g.
Carbohydrate:	20 g.
Fat:	7 g.
Cholesterol:	23 mg.
Sodium:	578 mg.
Exchanges:	1 starch,
	1 medium-fat meat,
	1 vegetable, ½ fat

French Onion & Beef Soup

2 large onions, sliced and separated into rings (about 2 cups)
2 tablespoons margarine or butter
½ lb. lean ground beef, crumbled
1 can (10½ oz.) condensed French onion soup
1½ cups hot water
4 slices French bread, ½ inch thick, toasted
1 cup shredded Swiss cheese

4 servings

In 3-quart casserole, combine onions and margarine. Cover. Microwave at High for 8 to 10 minutes, or until onions are soft and translucent, stirring once.

Add ground beef. Microwave at High, uncovered, for 2 to 4 minutes, or just until meat loses pink color, stirring once to break apart. Add soup and water. Mix well. Cover. Microwave at High for 4 to 6 minutes, or until soup is hot.

Ladle soup into 4 soup bowls. Top with toasted bread slices. Sprinkle evenly with cheese. Arrange bowls in microwave oven. Microwave at High for 4 to 5 minutes, or until cheese melts, rearranging bowls once or twice.

Per Serving:			
Calories:	381	Cholesterol:	61 mg.
Protein:	23 g.	Sodium:	915 mg.
Carbohydrate:	22 g.	Exchanges:	1 starch, 1 high-fat meat,
Fat:	23 g.		1½ medium-fat meat, 1½ vegetable, 1 fat

Greek-style Beef & Spinach Soup

½ lb. lean ground beef,
   crumbled
¼ cup sliced green onions
2 cans (14½ oz. each) ready-to-
   serve beef broth (3½ cups)
1 cup water
1 cup uncooked rosamarina
   (orzo) pasta
½ teaspoon dried oregano
   leaves
¼ teaspoon salt
2 cups torn fresh spinach
   leaves

4 to 6 servings

In 2-quart casserole, place ground beef and onions. Microwave at High for 2 to 4 minutes, or just until meat loses pink color, stirring once to break apart.

Add broth, water, pasta, oregano and salt. Mix well. Cover. Microwave at High for 10 to 20 minutes, or until pasta is tender, stirring once.

Add spinach. Mix well. Re-cover. Microwave at High for 2 to 3 minutes, or until spinach wilts and soup is hot, stirring once. Top individual servings with seeded chopped cucumber and tomatoes, and sliced black olives, if desired.

Per Serving:			
Calories:	113	Cholesterol:	29 mg.
Protein:	10 g.	Sodium:	571 mg.
Carbohydrate:	6 g.	Exchanges:	1 medium-fat meat, 1 vegetable
Fat:	6 g.		

Lentil Beef Soup

½ cup chopped carrot
½ cup chopped celery
½ cup chopped green pepper
½ cup chopped onion
¼ cup water
½ lb. lean ground beef,
    crumbled
2 cans (14½ oz. each) ready-
    to-serve chicken broth
    (3½ cups)
1 can (14½ oz.) diced
    tomatoes, undrained
¾ cup uncooked lentils
1 tablespoon dried parsley
    flakes
½ teaspoon salt
¼ teaspoon dried basil leaves
¼ teaspoon dried thyme leaves
1 bay leaf

6 to 8 servings

In 3-quart casserole, combine
carrot, celery, pepper, onion and
water. Cover. Microwave at High
for 5 to 7 minutes, or until vegetables are tender, stirring once.

Add ground beef. Microwave at
High, uncovered, for 2 to 4 minutes, or just until meat loses pink
color, stirring once to break apart.

Add remaining ingredients. Cover.
Microwave at High for 30 to 45
minutes, or until lentils are tender,
stirring twice. Remove and discard bay leaf.

Per Serving:	
Calories:	153
Protein:	13 g.
Carbohydrate:	15 g.
Fat:	5 g.
Cholesterol:	18 mg.
Sodium:	572 mg.
Exchanges:	½ starch,
	1 medium-fat meat,
	1½ vegetable

Beefy Tortilla Soup

4 corn tortillas (6-inch)
¼ cup vegetable oil
½ cup chopped celery
½ cup chopped red or green pepper
½ cup chopped onion
¼ cup water
½ lb. lean ground beef, crumbled
1 can (14½ oz.) ready-to-serve chicken broth (1¾ cups)
1 can (14½ oz.) diced tomatoes, undrained
1 can (8 oz.) corn, drained
1 avocado, peeled and cut into ½-inch chunks
2 tablespoons canned chopped green chilies
1½ teaspoons chili powder
¾ teaspoon cumin seed

6 servings

Per Serving:
Calories: 316
Protein: 12 g.
Carbohydrate: 28 g.
Fat: 19 g.
Cholesterol: 23 mg.
Sodium: 392 mg.
Exchanges: 1 starch,
1 medium-fat meat,
2½ vegetable, 2½ fat

How to Microwave Beefy Tortilla Soup

Cut tortillas into ¼-inch strips. Set aside. In 10-inch skillet, heat vegetable oil conventionally over medium heat.

Add tortilla strips. Fry until golden brown and crisp, about 3 to 5 minutes. Drain on paper towels. Set aside.

Combine celery, pepper, onion and water in 2-quart casserole. Cover. Microwave at High for 3 to 5 minutes, or until vegetables are tender, stirring once.

Add ground beef. Microwave at High, uncovered, for 2 to 4 minutes, or just until meat loses pink color, stirring once to break apart.

Add remaining ingredients. Cover. Microwave at High for 10 to 15 minutes, or until soup is hot, stirring once.

Divide tortilla strips evenly among 6 soup bowls. Ladle soup over tortilla strips. Serve immediately.

Italian Vegetable Soup

2 cups thinly sliced zucchini
  (about 8 oz.)
½ cup chopped onion
¼ cup water
½ lb. lean ground beef,
  crumbled
1 can (14½ oz.) ready-to-serve
  beef broth (1¾ cups)
1 cup spaghetti sauce
1 cup frozen sliced carrots
1 jar (6 oz.) whole mushrooms,
  drained
½ cup uncooked vermicelli
  pasta, broken into 2-inch
  lengths
¼ teaspoon Italian seasoning

6 servings

In 3-quart casserole, combine zucchini, onion and water. Cover. Microwave at High for 4 to 6 minutes, or until vegetables are tender, stirring once.

Add ground beef. Microwave at High, uncovered, for 2 to 4 minutes, or just until meat loses pink color, stirring once to break apart.

Add remaining ingredients. Mix well. Cover. Microwave at High for 15 to 25 minutes, or until pasta is tender, stirring once or twice.

Per Serving:
Calories:	160
Protein:	10 g.
Carbohydrate:	16 g.
Fat:	6 g.
Cholesterol:	23 mg.
Sodium:	641 mg.
Exchanges:	½ starch,
	1 medium-fat meat,
	1½ vegetable

Baked Bean & Beef Soup

½ cup chopped onion
½ cup chopped green pepper
1 cup plus 2 tablespoons water,
  divided
½ lb. lean ground beef,
  crumbled

1 can (21 oz.) baked beans
  seasoned with bacon
1 can (10¾ oz.) condensed
  tomato soup
1 can (8 oz.) corn, drained

6 servings

In 2-quart casserole, combine onion, pepper and 2 tablespoons water. Cover. Microwave at High for 3 to 4 minutes, or until vegetables are tender, stirring once.

Add ground beef. Microwave at High, uncovered, for 2 to 4 minutes, or just until meat loses pink color, stirring once to break apart.

Add remaining 1 cup water and remaining ingredients. Mix well. Cover with wax paper. Microwave at High for 5 to 10 minutes, or until soup is hot, stirring once.

Per Serving:
Calories:	263	Cholesterol:	27 mg.
Protein:	15 g.	Sodium:	940 mg.
Carbohydrate:	33 g.	Exchanges:	1½ starch, 1 medium-fat meat,
Fat:	9 g.		2 vegetable, ½ fat

Western-style Hamburger Soup

½ cup chopped celery
½ cup chopped onion
2 cups plus 2 tablespoons
  water, divided
¼ teaspoon instant minced
  garlic
½ lb. lean ground beef,
  crumbled
1 can (16 oz.) whole tomatoes,
  undrained and cut up
1 cup frozen sliced carrots
1 cup uncooked wagon wheel
  pasta
¼ cup barbecue sauce
1 tablespoon Worcestershire
  sauce
¼ teaspoon pepper
1 bay leaf

6 servings

In 3-quart casserole, combine celery, onion, 2 tablespoons water and the garlic. Cover. Microwave at High for 2 to 4 minutes, or until vegetables are tender.

Add ground beef. Microwave at High, uncovered, for 2 to 4 minutes, or just until meat loses pink color, stirring once to break apart.

Add remaining 2 cups water and remaining ingredients. Cover. Microwave at High for 20 to 30 minutes, or until pasta is tender, stirring twice. Remove and discard bay leaf.

Per Serving:
Calories: 138
Protein: 9 g.
Carbohydrate: 13 g.
Fat: 6 g.
Cholesterol: 29 mg.
Sodium: 273 mg.
Exchanges: ½ starch,
                  1 medium-fat meat,
                  1½ vegetable, ½ fat

Teriyaki Beef Soup

½ lb. lean ground beef,
    crumbled
½ teaspoon instant minced
    garlic
2 cans (14½ oz. each) ready-to-
    serve beef broth (3½ cups)
1 cup frozen sliced carrots
1 pkg. (6 oz.) frozen snow
    pea pods
1 can (4 oz.) mushroom pieces
    and stems, drained
1 pkg. (3 oz.) beef-flavor
    Oriental dry noodle soup
    mix (discard seasoning
    packet)
¼ cup teriyaki sauce

6 servings

In medium mixing bowl, combine ground beef and garlic. Mix well. Shape into 30 meatballs, about ½ inch in diameter. Set aside.

In 3-quart casserole, microwave broth at High, covered, for 5 to 11 minutes, or just until broth begins to boil.

Add meatballs, carrots, peas and mushrooms. Crumble noodles into broth. Add teriyaki sauce. Mix well. Re-cover. Microwave at High for 8 to 15 minutes, or until meatballs are firm and no longer pink and noodles are tender, stirring twice.

Per Serving:			
Calories:	183	Cholesterol:	37 mg.
Protein:	13 g.	Sodium:	1038 mg.
Carbohydrate:	19 g.	Exchanges:	1 starch, 1 medium-fat meat,
Fat:	6 g.		1 vegetable

Southern-style Gumbo ▶

¼ cup all-purpose flour
¼ cup vegetable oil
½ lb. lean ground beef,
   crumbled
1 can (14½ oz.) stewed
   tomatoes, undrained
1 can (14½ oz.) ready-to-serve
   chicken broth (1¾ cups)
1 pkg. (10 oz.) frozen sliced
   okra
⅔ cup uncooked instant rice
2 teaspoons dried parsley
   flakes
½ teaspoon instant minced
   garlic
¼ teaspoon salt
⅛ to ¼ teaspoon cayenne
⅛ teaspoon pepper

4 servings

Heat conventional oven to 400°F. Combine flour and oil in 8-inch square baking pan. Bake for 7 to 10 minutes, or until flour is deep golden brown, stirring every 5 minutes. Set aside.

In 2-quart casserole, microwave ground beef at High for 2 to 4 minutes, or just until meat loses pink color, stirring once to break apart. Add flour mixture and re-maining ingredients. Mix well. Cover. Microwave at High for 15 to 20 minutes, or until rice is ten-der and gumbo thickens and bubbles, stirring twice.

Per Serving:
Calories:	344
Protein:	16 g.
Carbohydrate:	22 g.
Fat:	22 g.
Cholesterol:	35 mg.
Sodium:	755 mg.
Exchanges:	1 starch, 1½ medium-fat meat, 1½ vegetable, 2½ fat

Bean, Beef & Bacon Soup

6 slices bacon
½ cup chopped onion
2 teaspoons vegetable oil
¼ teaspoon instant minced
   garlic
½ lb. lean ground beef,
   crumbled

2 cans (15 oz. each) navy
   beans, rinsed and drained
1 can (14½ oz.) diced
   tomatoes, undrained
1 can (14½ oz.) ready-to-serve
   beef broth (1¾ cups)
¼ cup tomato paste
½ teaspoon dried basil leaves

6 to 8 servings

Layer 3 paper towels on plate. Arrange bacon on paper towels. Cover with another paper towel. Microwave at High for 3 to 7 minutes, or until bacon is brown and crisp, rotating plate once. Let cool. Crumble. Set aside.

In 3-quart casserole, combine onion, oil and garlic. Cover. Microwave at High for 3 to 4 minutes, or until onion is tender, stirring once.

Add ground beef. Microwave at High, uncovered, for 2 to 4 minutes, or just until meat loses pink color, stirring once to break apart.

Add remaining ingredients. Cover. Microwave at High for 10 to 15 min-utes, or until soup is hot, stirring twice. Sprinkle each serving with 1 tablespoon crumbled bacon.

Per Serving:
Calories:	213	Cholesterol:	22 mg.
Protein:	14 g.	Sodium:	408 mg.
Carbohydrate:	22 g.	Exchanges:	1 starch, 1 medium-fat meat,
Fat:	8 g.		1½ vegetable, ½ fat

Stews

◀ Shipwrecked Stew

½ lb. lean ground beef,
   crumbled
1 medium onion, thinly sliced
   and separated into rings
½ cup chopped green pepper

½ teaspoon dried thyme leaves,
   divided
1 can (28 oz.) whole tomatoes,
   undrained and cut up
1 can (16 oz.) sliced potatoes,
   rinsed and drained

1 can (15½ oz.) kidney beans,
   rinsed and drained
1 can (14½ oz.) ready-to-serve
   beef broth (1¾ cups)
2 teaspoons chili powder
¼ teaspoon salt

6 to 8 servings

In 3-quart casserole, combine ground beef, onion, pepper and ¼ teaspoon thyme. Cover. Microwave at High for 7 to 9 minutes, or until onion is tender, stirring twice to break meat apart.

Add remaining ¼ teaspoon thyme and remaining ingredients. Mix well. Re-cover. Microwave at High for 15 to 20 minutes, or until hot, stirring twice.

Per Serving:	
Calories:	150
Protein:	10 g.
Carbohydrate:	18 g.
Fat:	4 g.
Cholesterol:	18 mg.
Sodium:	511 mg.
Exchanges:	½ starch,
	½ medium-fat meat,
	2 vegetable, ½ fat

Chunky Beef Stew

3 cups tomato juice or spicy hot
   vegetable cocktail juice,
   divided
2 medium carrots, cut into 1-inch
   lengths (about 1 cup)
2 stalks celery, cut into 1-inch
   lengths (about 1 cup)

1 medium onion, cut into
   8 wedges
½ teaspoon salt
¼ teaspoon pepper
¼ teaspoon instant minced
   garlic

¼ cup all-purpose flour
2 cans (16 oz.) whole potatoes,
   rinsed and drained
½ lb. lean ground beef,
   crumbled
1 cup frozen peas

6 servings

In 3-quart casserole, combine ½ cup tomato juice, the carrots, celery, onion, salt, pepper and garlic. Mix well. Cover. Microwave at High for 13 to 18 minutes, or until vegetables are tender, stirring twice. Set aside.

In small mixing bowl, combine ½ cup tomato juice and the flour. Stir until smooth. Add flour mixture, remaining 2 cups tomato juice and remaining ingredients to vegetables. Mix well. Re-cover. Microwave at High for 10 to 12 minutes, or until meat is no longer pink and stew is thickened, stirring once or twice.

Per Serving:	
Calories:	240
Protein:	12 g.
Carbohydrate:	37 g.
Fat:	6 g.
Cholesterol:	23 mg.
Sodium:	1081 mg.
Exchanges:	2 starch, ½ lean meat,
	1½ vegetable, ½ fat

Beef Burgundy Stew

½ lb. lean ground beef, crumbled
8 oz. fresh mushrooms, quartered (about 2½ cups)
2 slices bacon, cut into ½-inch pieces
½ cup all-purpose flour
½ teaspoon dried marjoram leaves
¼ teaspoon garlic powder
¼ teaspoon pepper
2½ cups beef broth
⅓ cup red wine
2 tablespoons tomato paste
2 tablespoons Worcestershire sauce
1 pkg. (20 oz.) frozen stew vegetables

6 servings

Per Serving:
Calories: 226
Protein: 14 g.
Carbohydrate: 25 g.
Fat: 7 g.
Cholesterol: 25 mg.
Sodium: 522 mg.
Exchanges: 1 starch,
1 medium-fat meat,
2 vegetable, ½ fat

How to Microwave Beef Burgundy Stew

Combine ground beef, mushrooms and bacon in 3-quart casserole. Cover. Microwave at High for 6 to 8 minutes, or until mushrooms are tender and meat loses pink color, stirring once to break apart.

Stir in flour, marjoram, garlic powder and pepper. Blend in broth, wine, tomato paste and Worcestershire sauce.

Add vegetables. Mix well. Recover. Microwave at High for 15 to 25 minutes, or until stew thickens and bubbles, stirring twice.

Beef Ratatouille Stew

- 1 eggplant (1 lb.), cut into ½-inch chunks
- 1 medium zucchini (about 8 oz.), thinly sliced
- 1 medium onion, thinly sliced and separated into rings
- ½ medium red pepper, cut into thin strips (2 × ¼-inch)

- 2 tablespoons olive oil
- 2 tablespoons water
- 2 teaspoons dried parsley flakes
- 1 teaspoon dried basil leaves
- 1 teaspoon dried oregano leaves
- 1 teaspoon sugar

- 1 teaspoon salt
- ⅛ teaspoon pepper
- ½ lb. lean ground beef, crumbled
- 2 cans (16 oz. each) whole tomatoes, undrained and cut up

6 to 8 servings

In 3-quart casserole, combine all ingredients, except ground beef and tomatoes. Mix well. Cover. Microwave at High for 18 to 22 minutes, or until eggplant is translucent, stirring twice.

Add ground beef and tomatoes. Mix well. Re-cover. Microwave at High for 3 to 6 minutes, or until meat is firm and no longer pink and stew is hot, stirring once.

Per Serving:	
Calories:	135
Protein:	7 g.
Carbohydrate:	11 g.
Fat:	8 g.
Cholesterol:	18 mg.
Sodium:	471 mg.
Exchanges:	½ medium-fat meat, 2 vegetable, 1 fat

Main Dishes

Cajun Meatloaf

Meatloaves & Meatballs

◄ Saucy Italian Meatloaf

8 oz. uncooked fettucini
1½ lbs. lean ground beef, crumbled
½ cup seasoned dry bread crumbs

½ cup milk
1 egg
1 teaspoon Italian seasoning
½ teaspoon salt

¼ teaspoon pepper
¼ teaspoon garlic powder
1½ cups spaghetti sauce

8 servings

Per Serving:	
Calories:	353
Protein:	22 g.
Carbohydrate:	33 g.
Fat:	14 g.
Cholesterol:	88 mg.
Sodium:	560 mg.
Exchanges:	1½ starch, 2 medium-fat meat, 2 vegetable, 1 fat

Prepare fettucini as directed on package. Rinse and drain. Arrange in even layer on serving platter. Cover to keep warm. Set aside. In medium mixing bowl, combine remaining ingredients, except spaghetti sauce. Mix well. Shape mixture into loaf. Place in 8 × 4-inch loaf dish. Microwave at High for 15 to 22 minutes, or until meatloaf is firm and internal temperature registers 150°F in center, rotating twice. Let stand, covered with foil, for 5 minutes.

Place spaghetti sauce in 4-cup measure. Cover with wax paper. Microwave at High for 3 to 4 minutes, or until hot, stirring once. Slice meatloaf. Arrange slices over cooked fettucini. Spoon spaghetti sauce over meatloaf slices and noodles.

Cajun Meatloaf

¼ cup all-purpose flour
¼ cup vegetable oil

Meatloaf:
1½ lbs. lean ground beef, crumbled
½ cup finely chopped green pepper
½ cup unseasoned dry bread crumbs

¼ cup chili sauce
1 egg
1 tablespoon Worcestershire sauce
1 tablespoon instant minced onion
½ to ¾ teaspoon cayenne
½ teaspoon salt
½ teaspoon pepper

¼ teaspoon instant minced garlic
¾ cup beef broth
¼ cup finely chopped red pepper
⅛ teaspoon black pepper
⅛ teaspoon garlic powder
Dash to ⅛ teaspoon cayenne

8 servings

Per Serving:	
Calories:	291
Protein:	18 g.
Carbohydrate:	11 g.
Fat:	19 g.
Cholesterol:	87 mg.
Sodium:	443 mg.
Exchanges:	2 medium-fat meat, 2 vegetable, 2 fat

Heat conventional oven to 400°F. Combine flour and oil in 8-inch square baking pan. Bake for 7 to 10 minutes, or until flour is deep golden brown, stirring every 5 minutes. Set aside.

In medium mixing bowl, combine all meatloaf ingredients. Mix well. Shape mixture into loaf. Place in 8 × 4-inch loaf dish. Microwave at High for 15 to 22 minutes, or until meatloaf is firm and internal temperature registers 150°F in center, rotating twice. Let stand, covered with foil, for 5 minutes.

In 4-cup measure, combine flour mixture and remaining ingredients. Mix well. Microwave at High for 3 to 3½ minutes, or until mixture thickens and bubbles, stirring every minute. Slice meatloaf and serve with gravy.

Creamy Herb Horseradish-sauced Meatloaf

Sauce:
¼ cup mayonnaise or salad dressing
¼ cup cream-style horseradish
¼ teaspoon dried parsley flakes
⅛ teaspoon dried basil leaves
⅛ teaspoon dried thyme leaves
⅛ teaspoon white pepper
Dash cayenne

Meatloaf:
1½ lbs. lean ground beef, crumbled
½ cup finely chopped red onion
½ cup finely chopped red or green pepper
½ cup snipped fresh parsley
1 egg
¼ cup unseasoned dry bread crumbs
1 tablespoon Worcestershire sauce
½ teaspoon salt
¼ teaspoon white pepper

8 servings

In small mixing bowl, combine all sauce ingredients. Mix well. Cover with plastic wrap. Chill.

In medium mixing bowl, combine all meatloaf ingredients. Mix well. Shape mixture into loaf. Place in 8 × 4-inch loaf dish. Microwave at High for 15 to 22 minutes, or until meatloaf is firm and internal temperature registers 150°F in center, rotating twice. Let stand, covered with foil, for 5 minutes. Slice and serve with sauce.

Per Serving:	
Calories:	248
Protein:	17 g.
Carbohydrate:	5 g.
Fat:	18 g.
Cholesterol:	91 mg.
Sodium:	281 mg.
Exchanges:	2 medium-fat meat, 1 vegetable, 1 fat

Southwestern Rolled Meatloaf ▲

Filling:
1 can (8 oz.) corn, drained
1 can (4 oz.) chopped green chilies, drained
½ cup shredded Monterey Jack cheese
¼ teaspoon salt

Meatloaf:
1½ lbs. lean ground beef, crumbled

½ cup unseasoned dry bread crumbs
½ cup spicy hot vegetable juice cocktail or tomato juice
1 tablespoon dried parsley flakes
¼ teaspoon salt

8 servings

In small mixing bowl, combine all filling ingredients. Mix well. Set aside. In medium mixing bowl, combine all meatloaf ingredients. Mix well. On wax paper, shape mixture into 12 × 8-inch rectangle. Spoon filling to within 1 inch of edges.

Roll up loaf, starting with short side. Lift paper until meat begins to roll tightly, enclosing filling. Continue to lift and peel back paper while completing the roll. Seal edges. Place meatloaf seam-side-down in 8 × 4-inch loaf dish. Microwave at High for 19 to 22 minutes, or until meatloaf is firm and internal temperature registers 150°F in center, rotating twice. Let stand, covered with foil, for 5 minutes.

Per Serving:			
Calories:	243	Cholesterol:	59 mg.
Protein:	18 g.	Sodium:	401 mg.
Carbohydrate:	11 g.	Exchanges:	½ starch, 2 medium-fat meat,
Fat:	14 g.		1 vegetable, ½ fat

Pot Roast-style Meatloaf*

Meatloaf:

1½ lbs. lean ground beef, crumbled
⅓ cup unseasoned dry bread crumbs
1 egg
¼ cup catsup or chili sauce
1 tablespoon instant minced onion

1 teaspoon Worcestershire sauce
½ teaspoon dry mustard
½ teaspoon salt
¼ teaspoon pepper

1 can (16 oz.) whole potatoes, rinsed and drained

1 cup frozen sliced carrots
1 cup sliced celery (½-inch slices)
½ cup frozen whole onions
1 pkg. (0.87 oz.) brown gravy mix
¾ cup water
¼ cup red wine

8 servings

In medium mixing bowl, combine all meatloaf ingredients. Mix well. Shape mixture into loaf. Place in 10-inch square casserole. Arrange potatoes, carrots, celery and onions around meatloaf. Set aside.

Place gravy mix in 2-cup measure. Blend in water and wine. Pour mixture over vegetables. Microwave at High for 28 to 30 minutes, or until meatloaf is firm and internal temperature registers 150°F in center, stirring vegetables 3 times and rotating casserole once. Let stand, covered with foil, for 10 minutes. Slice meatloaf and serve with vegetables and gravy.

*Recipe not recommended for ovens with less than 600 cooking watts.

Per Serving:	
Calories:	252
Protein:	18 g.
Carbohydrate:	16 g.
Fat:	12 g.
Cholesterol:	87 mg.
Sodium:	582 mg.
Exchanges:	½ starch, 2 medium-fat meat, 2 vegetable, ½ fat

Glazed Mini Meatloaves & Carrots

½ cup packed brown sugar
3 tablespoons cider vinegar
2 tablespoons Dijon mustard
1 pkg. (16 oz.) frozen whole
    baby carrots
¼ cup water

Meatloaf:

1 lb. lean ground beef,
    crumbled
⅓ cup sliced green onions
1 egg
¼ cup unseasoned dry bread
    crumbs
1 tablespoon soy sauce
1 tablespoon milk
½ teaspoon salt

4 servings

In 1-cup measure, combine sugar, vinegar and mustard. Mix well. Set aside. In 2-quart casserole, combine carrots and water. Cover. Microwave at High for 8 to 12 minutes, or until carrots are hot, stirring once. Drain. Pour half of sugar mixture over carrots. Set remaining sugar mixture aside. Toss to coat carrots. Set aside.

In medium mixing bowl, combine all meatloaf ingredients. Mix well. Divide mixture into 4 equal portions. Shape each portion into 4 × 2½-inch loaf. Place on roasting rack. Brush tops of meatloaves with half of remaining sugar mixture.

Microwave at High for 7 to 8 minutes, or until meatloaves are firm and no longer pink, turning once and brushing with remaining sugar mixture. Let stand, covered with foil, for 5 minutes. While meatloaves stand, reheat carrots at High for 2 to 3 minutes, or until hot, stirring once. Serve carrots with slotted spoon.

Per Serving:			
Calories:	429	Cholesterol:	139 mg.
Protein:	24 g.	Sodium:	991 mg.
Carbohydrate:	43 g.	Exchanges:	2½ medium-fat meat,
Fat:	17 g.		2½ vegetable, 2 fruit, 1 fat

Cornmeal-crusted Sloppy Joe Loaf

2 tablespoons yellow cornmeal
1 pkg. (10 oz.) refrigerated pizza
     crust dough
1 lb. lean ground beef,
     crumbled
1 can (8 oz.) whole tomatoes,
     undrained and cut up
1 pkg. (1.5 oz.) sloppy joe
     seasoning mix
2 teaspoons prepared mustard
1 teaspoon white vinegar

6 servings

Per Serving:	
Calories:	300
Protein:	18 g.
Carbohydrate:	29 g.
Fat:	12 g.
Cholesterol:	47 mg.
Sodium:	855 mg.
Exchanges:	1½ starch, 1½ medium-fat meat, 1½ vegetable, 1 fat

How to Make Cornmeal-crusted Sloppy Joe Loaf

Heat conventional oven to 425°F. Sprinkle cornmeal on large baking sheet. Remove dough from package. Unroll dough and place on prepared baking sheet. Press out dough, starting at center, to form 15 × 10-inch rectangle. Set dough aside.

Place ground beef in 2-quart casserole. Microwave at High for 4 to 7 minutes, or until meat is no longer pink, stirring twice to break apart. Drain. Add remaining ingredients. Mix well. Microwave at High for 2 to 4 minutes, or until mixture is slightly thickened and liquid is absorbed, stirring once.

Spoon mixture in 4-inch strip lengthwise down center of dough. Cut dough diagonally at 1-inch intervals to within ½ inch of filling. Bring alternate strips over filling, overlapping strips at center, for braided effect. Bake for 10 to 15 minutes, or until light golden brown. Serve in slices.

Chili-sauced Meatballs

Meatballs:
- 1 lb. lean ground beef, crumbled
- ½ cup corn bread stuffing mix
- 1 egg
- 2 teaspoons instant minced onion
- ½ teaspoon chili powder
- ¼ teaspoon garlic salt

Sauce:
- ½ cup chopped green pepper
- 1 can (15 oz.) chili beans in chili sauce, undrained
- 1 can (14½ oz.) diced tomatoes, undrained
- 1 teaspoon chili powder
- ½ teaspoon sugar

- 3 cups hot cooked long-grain white rice (1 cup uncooked)

4 to 6 servings

In medium mixing bowl, combine all meatball ingredients. Mix well. Shape into 16 meatballs, about 1½ inches in diameter. Set aside.

Place pepper in 2-quart casserole. Cover. Microwave at High for 1 to 2 minutes, or until tender-crisp. Add remaining sauce ingredients. Re-cover. Microwave at High for 4 to 6 minutes, or until sauce is hot, stirring twice.

Add meatballs to sauce. Stir gently to coat with sauce. Re-cover. Microwave at High for 8 to 10 minutes, or until meatballs are firm and no longer pink, stirring gently to rearrange 2 or 3 times. Serve over rice.

Per Serving:	
Calories:	415
Protein:	23 g.
Carbohydrate:	46 g.
Fat:	16 g.
Cholesterol:	105 mg.
Sodium:	774 mg.
Exchanges:	2 starch, 2 medium-fat meat, 3 vegetable, 1 fat

Spaghetti with Meatballs

Meatballs:
- 1 lb. lean ground beef, crumbled
- ⅓ cup unseasoned dry bread crumbs
- 1 egg
- ¼ cup grated Parmesan cheese
- 2 teaspoons instant minced onion
- ¼ teaspoon salt
- ⅛ teaspoon pepper

Sauce:
- 1 can (28 oz.) Roma tomatoes, undrained and cut up
- 2 cups water
- 2 cans (6 oz. each) tomato paste
- 1 tablespoon sugar
- 1 tablespoon instant minced onion
- 1 teaspoon salt

- 1 teaspoon dried oregano leaves
- ½ teaspoon dried basil leaves
- ½ teaspoon pepper
- ¼ teaspoon instant minced garlic
- 1 bay leaf

- 12 oz. hot cooked spaghetti

6 servings

In medium mixing bowl, combine all meatball ingredients. Mix well. Shape into 16 meatballs, about 1½ inches in diameter. Set aside.

In 3-quart casserole, combine all sauce ingredients. Mix well. Add meatballs to sauce. Stir gently to coat with sauce. Cover with wax paper. Microwave at High for 20 to 30 minutes, or until meatballs are firm and no longer pink, stirring gently to rearrange 3 times. Remove and discard bay leaf. Serve over spaghetti.

Per Serving:	
Calories:	311
Protein:	18 g.
Carbohydrate:	38 g.
Fat:	10 g.
Cholesterol:	72 mg.
Sodium:	960 mg.
Exchanges:	1½ starch, 1 medium-fat meat, 3 vegetable, 1 fat

Curried Meatballs

4   new potatoes, cut lengthwise
     into quarters (about 10 oz.)
1   cup thinly sliced carrots
¼   cup water
1   pkg. (10 oz.) frozen
     asparagus cuts

Meatballs:

1   lb. lean ground beef,
     crumbled
⅓   cup unseasoned dry bread
     crumbs
⅓   cup sliced green onions
1   egg
¼   teaspoon salt
¼   teaspoon instant minced
     garlic

⅓   cup all-purpose flour
1   tablespoon curry powder
⅛   teaspoon cayenne
2   cups chicken broth
3   cups hot cooked long-grain
     white rice (1 cup uncooked)

4 to 6 servings

In 3-quart casserole, combine potatoes, carrots and water. Cover. Microwave at High for 8 to 10 minutes, or until potatoes are tender, stirring once. Add asparagus. Re-cover. Microwave at High for 5 to 7 minutes, or until asparagus is hot, stirring once to break apart. Drain. Set aside.

In medium mixing bowl, combine all meatball ingredients. Mix well. Shape into 16 meatballs, about 1½ inches in diameter. Arrange meatballs in single layer in 8-inch square baking dish. Microwave at High for 6 to 8 minutes, or until meatballs are firm and no longer pink, rearranging once. Drain. Add meatballs to vegetable mixture. Set aside.

In 4-cup measure, combine flour, curry powder and cayenne. Blend in broth. Microwave at High for 4 to 6 minutes, or until sauce thickens and bubbles, stirring after the first 2 minutes and then every minute. Add to vegetable mixture. Toss to coat. If necessary, microwave mixture at High for 1 to 2 minutes to reheat. Serve over rice.

Per Serving:			
Calories:	396	Cholesterol:	93 mg.
Protein:	22 g.	Sodium:	456 mg.
Carbohydrate:	49 g.	Exchanges:	2½ starch, 1½ medium-fat meat,
Fat:	12 g.		2 vegetable, 1½ fat

Portuguese Meatballs with Rice

2 cups plus 2 tablespoons water, divided
1 cup uncooked long-grain white rice
1½ teaspoons salt, divided
¼ teaspoon ground turmeric
1 cup green pepper chunks (1-inch chunks)
½ cup coarsely chopped onion
2 cups seeded chopped tomatoes
½ cup sliced black olives
1 lb. lean ground beef, crumbled
1 egg
⅓ cup unseasoned dry bread crumbs
1 tablespoon instant minced onion
½ teaspoon dried parsley flakes
¼ teaspoon ground cinnamon
¼ teaspoon ground cumin
¼ teaspoon pepper
½ cup oil and vinegar dressing

4 to 6 servings

In 2-quart saucepan, combine 2 cups water, the rice, 1 teaspoon salt and the turmeric. Mix well. Heat conventionally over medium-high heat, until water begins to boil. Reduce heat to low. Cover. Simmer for 15 to 20 minutes, or until rice is tender and liquid is absorbed. Fluff with fork. Set aside, covered, to keep warm.

In 3-quart casserole, combine green pepper, onion and remaining 2 tablespoons water. Mix well. Cover. Microwave at High for 4 to 5 minutes, or until pepper chunks are tender-crisp, stirring once. Drain. Add tomatoes and olives. Mix well. Set aside.

In large mixing bowl, combine remaining ½ teaspoon salt and remaining ingredients, except dressing. Mix well. Shape into 16 meatballs, about 1½ inches in diameter. Arrange meatballs in single layer in 8-inch square baking dish. Microwave at High for 6 to 8 minutes, or until meatballs are firm and no longer pink, rearranging once. Drain. Add meatballs and dressing to vegetable mixture. Toss to combine. Serve over rice.

Per Serving:			
Calories:	421	Cholesterol:	93 mg.
Protein:	18 g.	Sodium:	1001 mg.
Carbohydrate:	36 g.	Exchanges:	1½ starch, 1½ medium-fat meat,
Fat:	22 g.		2½ vegetable, 3 fat

Entrées

◄ Hamburger Steaks with Vegetable Salsa

Hamburger Steaks:
- 1 lb. lean ground beef, crumbled
- ¼ cup picante salsa sauce
- ¼ cup unseasoned dry bread crumbs
- 1 egg
- ½ teaspoon dried oregano leaves
- ¼ teaspoon garlic powder

Salsa:
- 1 cup frozen corn
- 1 cup cubed zucchini (½-inch cubes)
- 1 cup seeded chopped tomato
- ⅓ cup sliced green onions
- ¼ cup picante salsa sauce
- 1 tablespoon olive oil or vegetable oil
- ¼ teaspoon salt

4 servings

In medium mixing bowl, combine all hamburger steak ingredients. Mix well. Divide mixture into 4 equal portions. Shape each portion into 4-inch round patty. Arrange on roasting rack. Set aside.

In 2-quart casserole, combine all salsa ingredients. Cover. Microwave at High for 6 to 8 minutes, or until mixture is hot, stirring once or twice. Set aside, covered, to keep warm.

Microwave hamburger steaks at High for 7 to 10 minutes, or until meat is firm and no longer pink, turning once. Let stand, covered with wax paper, for 2 minutes. Serve hamburger steaks topped with salsa.

Per Serving:			
Calories:	358	Cholesterol:	139 mg.
Protein:	24 g.	Sodium:	495 mg.
Carbohydrate:	19 g.	Exchanges:	1 starch, 2½ medium-fat meat,
Fat:	20 g.		1 vegetable, 1½ fat

Vegetable Gravy-topped Burgers

Burgers:
- 1 lb. lean ground beef, crumbled
- ½ cup unseasoned dry bread crumbs
- 1 egg
- ¼ cup milk
- ½ teaspoon salt
- ¼ teaspoon pepper
- ¼ teaspoon garlic powder

Gravy:
- 1 cup beef broth
- 1 tablespoon plus 1 teaspoon cornstarch
- 1½ cups julienne carrots (2 × ½-inch strips)
- 1 cup sliced fresh mushrooms
- 1 medium onion, sliced and separated into rings
- 2 tablespoons snipped fresh parsley

In medium mixing bowl, combine all burger ingredients. Mix well. Divide mixture into 4 equal portions. Shape each portion into 4-inch round patty. Arrange on roasting rack. Set aside.

In 2-quart casserole, combine broth and cornstarch. Mix well. Add remaining ingredients. Cover. Microwave at High for 8 to 10 minutes, or until gravy is thickened and translucent, stirring once. Set aside, covered, to keep warm.

Microwave patties at High for 7 to 10 minutes, or until meat is firm and no longer pink, turning once. Let stand, covered with wax paper, for 2 minutes. Serve burgers topped with gravy.

Per Serving:			
Calories:	342	Cholesterol:	141 mg.
Protein:	25 g.	Sodium:	657 mg.
Carbohydrate:	20 g.	Exchanges:	½ starch, 2½ medium-fat meat,
Fat:	17 g.		2½ vegetable, 1 fat

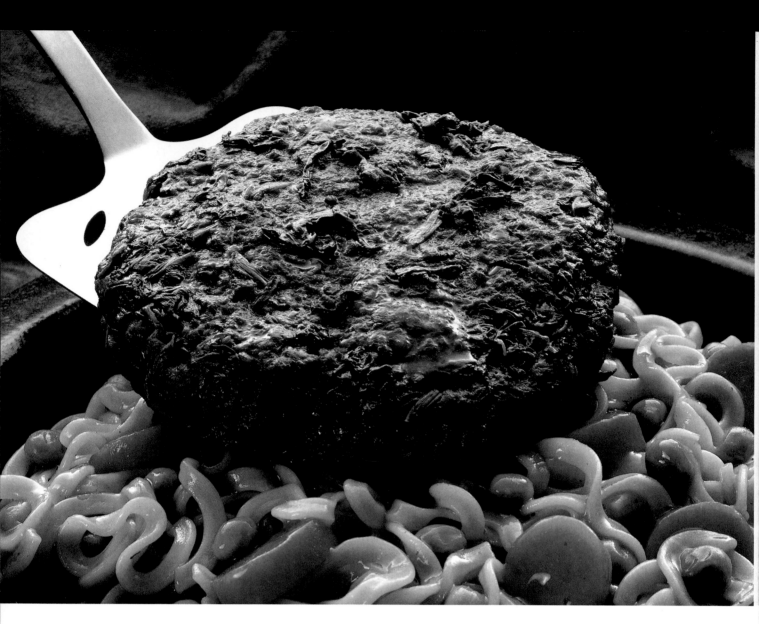

Vegetable Burgers with Saucy Noodles

4 oz. uncooked medium egg
  noodles (about 2 cups)
1 cup frozen sliced carrots
1 cup frozen peas
½ cup prepared beef gravy
1 pkg. (10 oz.) frozen chopped
  spinach
1 lb. lean ground beef,
  crumbled
1 cup herb-seasoned stuffing
  mix
½ cup milk
1 egg
½ teaspoon dried rubbed sage
  leaves
¼ teaspoon pepper

4 servings

Prepare noodles as directed on package. Rinse and drain. Set aside.

In 2-quart casserole, combine carrots, peas and gravy. Mix well. Cover. Microwave at High for 5 to 7 minutes, or until vegetables are hot, stirring once. Add noodles to mixture. Toss to combine. Set aside, covered, to keep warm.

Unwrap spinach and place on plate. Microwave at High for 4 to 6 minutes, or until defrosted. Drain, pressing to remove excess moisture.

In large mixing bowl, combine spinach and remaining ingredients. Mix well. Divide mixture into 4 equal portions. Shape each portion into 4-inch round patty. Arrange on roasting rack. Microwave at High for 13 to 15 minutes, or until meat is firm and no longer pink, turning once.

Let stand, covered with wax paper, for 2 minutes. To serve, spoon vegetable mixture evenly onto each plate. Top with burger. Serve immediately.

Per Serving:			
Calories:	569	Cholesterol:	171 mg.
Protein:	36 g.	Sodium:	690 mg.
Carbohydrate:	60 g.	Exchanges:	3 starch, 3 medium-fat meat,
Fat:	21 g.		3 vegetable, 1 fat

Mushroom-sauced Stacked Hash

1 pkg. (12 oz.) frozen hash
   brown patties

Burgers:
1 lb. lean ground beef, crumbled
¼ cup sliced green onions
¼ cup chopped green pepper
¼ cup chopped red pepper
1 egg
2 tablespoons unseasoned dry
   bread crumbs
1 tablespoon red wine
   (optional)
1 teaspoon Worcestershire
   sauce
¼ teaspoon garlic powder

1 pkg. (0.87 oz.) brown gravy
   mix
1 cup cold water
1 can (4 oz.) mushroom pieces
   and stems, drained

4 servings

Prepare hash brown patties as directed on package. Place on serving platter. Cover with foil to keep warm. Set aside.

In medium mixing bowl, combine all burger ingredients. Mix well. Divide mixture into 4 equal portions. Shape each portion into 5 × 3-inch patty. Arrange on roasting rack. Microwave at High for 7 to 10 minutes, or until meat is firm and no longer pink, turning once. Let stand, covered with wax paper.

Place gravy mix in 4-cup measure. Blend in water. Microwave at High for 3 to 4 minutes, or until gravy is thickened and translucent, stirring with whisk after first 2 minutes and then every minute. Add mushrooms to gravy. Place burgers on top of hash brown patties. Top evenly with gravy.

Per Serving:			
Calories:	356	Cholesterol:	139 mg.
Protein:	25 g.	Sodium:	544 mg.
Carbohydrate:	24 g.	Exchanges:	1 starch, 2½ medium-fat meat,
Fat:	18 g.		2 vegetable, 1 fat

Greek Stuffed Potatoes

1   carton (8 oz.) plain yogurt
½   cup seeded finely chopped
      cucumber
4   medium baking potatoes
      (8 to 10 oz. each)
½   lb. lean ground beef,
      crumbled
½   cup seeded chopped tomato
¼   cup plus 1 tablespoon sliced
      green onions, divided
2   tablespoons catsup
1   teaspoon dried parsley flakes
¼   teaspoon dried oregano
      leaves
¼   teaspoon garlic salt

4 servings

In small mixing bowl, combine yogurt and cucumber. Mix well. Set aside. Pierce potatoes with fork. Arrange in circle on paper towel in microwave oven. Microwave at High for 10 to 16 minutes, or just until tender, rearranging once. Let stand for 10 minutes.

In 1-quart casserole, microwave ground beef at High for 2 to 4 minutes, or until meat is no longer pink, stirring once to break apart. Drain. Add tomato, ¼ cup onions and remaining ingredients. Mix well.

Arrange potatoes on serving plate. Slash each potato lengthwise and then crosswise. Gently press both ends until center pops open. Spoon meat mixture evenly into center of each potato. Serve topped with yogurt mixture. Sprinkle evenly with remaining 1 tablespoon onion.

Per Serving:			
Calories:	282	Cholesterol:	39 mg.
Protein:	17 g.	Sodium:	288 mg.
Carbohydrate:	35 g.	Exchanges:	2 starch, 1½ medium-fat meat,
Fat:	9 g.		1 vegetable

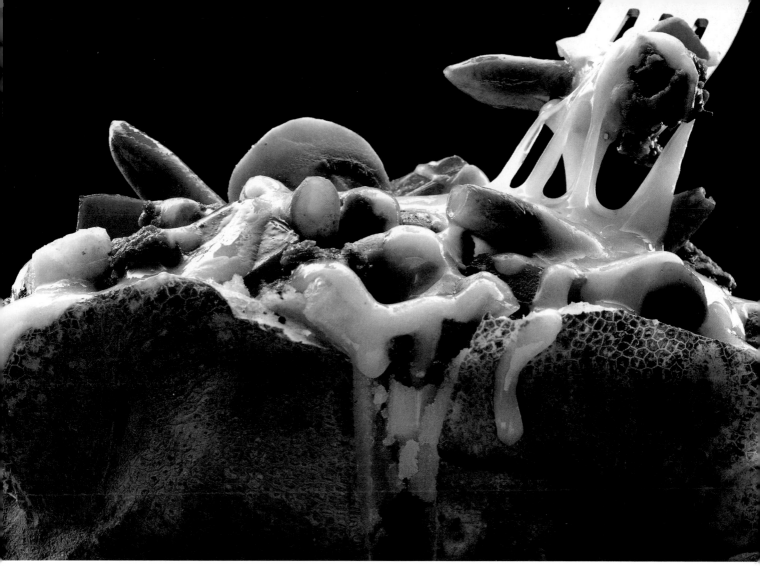

Italian Stuffed Potatoes

4 medium baking potatoes
   (8 to 10 oz. each)
1 pkg. (9 oz.) frozen cut green
   beans
1 cup sliced fresh mushrooms
½ lb. lean ground beef,
   crumbled
¼ cup chopped onion
1 cup seeded chopped tomato
2 tablespoons tomato paste
¼ teaspoon dried basil leaves
¼ teaspoon dried thyme leaves
¼ teaspoon garlic powder
¼ teaspoon salt
¼ teaspoon pepper
½ cup shredded mozzarella
   cheese

4 servings

Pierce potatoes with fork. Arrange in circle on paper towel in microwave oven. Microwave at High for 10 to 16 minutes, or just until tender, re-arranging once. Let stand for 10 minutes.

In 2-quart casserole, combine green beans and mushrooms. Cover. Microwave at High for 6 to 8 minutes, or until beans are hot, stirring once to break apart. Drain. Set aside.

In 1-quart casserole, combine ground beef and onion. Mix well. Micro-wave at High for 2 to 4 minutes, or until meat is no longer pink, stirring once. Drain. Add ground beef and remaining ingredients, except cheese, to vegetable mixture. Mix well. Set aside.

Arrange potatoes on serving plate. Slash each potato lengthwise and then crosswise. Gently press both ends until center pops open. Spoon meat mixture evenly into center of each potato. Sprinkle evenly with cheese. Microwave at High for 2 to 4 minutes, or until cheese melts, rotating dish once.

Per Serving:			
Calories:	313	Cholesterol:	43 mg.
Protein:	19 g.	Sodium:	320 mg.
Carbohydrate:	38 g.	Exchanges:	2 starch, 1½ medium-fat meat,
Fat:	10 g.		1½ vegetable, ½ fat

Shepherd's Stuffed Potatoes

4 medium baking potatoes
(8 to 10 oz. each)

Meat Mixture:

½ lb. lean ground beef, crumbled

1 cup frozen mixed vegetables or peas

½ cup prepared beef or brown gravy

½ teaspoon instant minced onion

¼ teaspoon garlic powder

¼ teaspoon salt

⅓ cup milk

1 tablespoon margarine or butter

¼ teaspoon salt

¼ teaspoon pepper

¼ cup shredded Cheddar cheese

4 servings

Per Serving:
Calories:	336
Protein:	18 g.
Carbohydrate:	35 g.
Fat:	14 g.
Cholesterol:	45 mg.
Sodium:	428 mg.
Exchanges:	2 starch, 1½ medium-fat meat, 1 vegetable, 1 fat

How to Microwave Shepherd's Stuffed Potatoes

Pierce potatoes with fork. Arrange in circle on paper towel in microwave oven. Microwave at High for 10 to 16 minutes, or just until tender, rearranging once. Let stand for 10 minutes.

Place ground beef in 1-quart casserole. Microwave at High for 2 to 4 minutes, or until no longer pink, stirring once to break apart. Drain. Add remaining meat mixture ingredients. Mix well.

Microwave at High for 3 to 4 minutes, or until hot, stirring once. Set aside, covered. Cut thin slice from top of each potato. Scoop out pulp, leaving ¼-inch shell. Place pulp in medium mixing bowl.

Set shells aside. Add remaining ingredients, except cheese, to pulp. Beat at medium speed of electric mixer until smooth and fluffy.

Spoon meat mixture evenly into potato shells. Spoon or pipe mashed potatoes evenly over meat mixture in each potato shell. Arrange potatoes on serving plate.

Sprinkle evenly with cheese. Microwave at High for 5 to 6 minutes, or until potatoes are hot and cheese is melted, rotating plate once.

Spicy Hamburger Stew in Polenta Ring ▶

3¼ cups hot water
¼ teaspoon salt
1½ cups yellow cornmeal
2 tablespoons snipped fresh parsley
1 tablespoon margarine or butter
1 lb. lean ground beef, coarsely crumbled
1 small onion, cut into thin wedges
1 can (16 oz.) whole potatoes, rinsed and drained, cut in half
1 pkg. (10 oz.) frozen peas and carrots
¼ cup plus 2 tablespoons all-purpose flour
½ teaspoon ground cumin
¼ teaspoon caraway seed
¼ teaspoon pepper
⅛ teaspoon cayenne
1 can (16 oz.) whole tomatoes, undrained and cut up
1 can (10½ oz.) condensed beef broth
2 tablespoons tomato paste

6 to 8 servings

In 2-quart casserole, place water and salt. Cover. Microwave at High for 8 to 12 minutes, or until water boils. Add cornmeal, parsley and margarine gradually, stirring constantly with whisk until mixture is smooth.

Microwave, uncovered, at High for 2 to 4 minutes, or until mixture is very thick, stirring once or twice. Spoon mixture into 4-cup glass ring mold. Cover with plastic wrap. Set aside.

In 3-quart casserole, microwave ground beef and onion at High for 4 to 7 minutes, or until meat is no longer pink, stirring once or twice. Drain. Add potatoes and peas and carrots. Stir to break apart frozen vegetables. Set aside.

In small mixing bowl, combine flour, cumin, caraway seed, pepper and cayenne. Mix well. Stir flour mixture into meat and vegetables.

Add tomatoes, broth and tomato paste. Mix well. Cover. Microwave at High for 15 to 23 minutes, or until stew is very hot and thickened, stirring 2 or 3 times.

If necessary, reheat polenta ring at High for 1 to 2 minutes, or until hot. Loosen ring mold around edges and invert polenta ring onto serving platter. Spoon about 2 cups of stew mixture into center of ring. Serve polenta ring with remaining stew.

Per Serving:			
Calories:	287	Cholesterol:	35 mg.
Protein:	16 g.	Sodium:	482 mg.
Carbohydrate:	34 g.	Exchanges:	2 starch, 1 medium-fat meat,
Fat:	10 g.		1 vegetable, 1 fat

Quick & Easy Stuffed Peppers

2 large green, red or yellow peppers (8 oz. each)
¼ cup water
1 lb. lean ground beef, crumbled
½ cup chopped onion
1 cup hot cooked long-grain white rice (⅓ cup uncooked)
1 can (8 oz.) whole tomatoes, undrained and cut up
1 can (6 oz.) tomato paste
1 teaspoon sugar
¼ teaspoon dried basil leaves
¼ teaspoon salt
½ cup shredded Cheddar cheese

4 servings

Cut each pepper in half lengthwise. Remove stem, seeds and membrane. Place water in 8-inch square baking dish. Arrange pepper halves cut-sides-up in dish. Cover with plastic wrap. Microwave at High for 5 to 7 minutes, or until tender-crisp, rearranging once. Drain. Set aside.

In 2-quart casserole, microwave ground beef and onion at High for 4 to 7 minutes, or until meat is no longer pink, stirring twice to break apart. Drain. Add remaining ingredients, except cheese. Mix well.

Spoon meat mixture evenly into peppers, mounding slightly. Re-cover. Microwave at High for 7 to 10 minutes, or until peppers are tender and meat mixture is firm and hot, rotating dish and rearranging peppers twice. Sprinkle cheese evenly over peppers. Re-cover. Let stand for 2 minutes, or until cheese is melted.

Per Serving:			
Calories:	410	Cholesterol:	85 mg.
Protein:	28 g.	Sodium:	627 mg.
Carbohydrate:	30 g.	Exchanges:	1 starch, 2½ medium-fat meat,
Fat:	21 g.		3 vegetable, 1½ fat

◄ Herb-crusted Calzones

1	pkg. (16 oz.) hot roll mix
1¼	cups hot water (120°F to 130°F)
3	tablespoons plus 1 teaspoon olive oil or vegetable oil, divided
½	lb. lean ground beef, crumbled
1	can (8 oz.) tomato sauce
1	cup shredded mozzerella cheese
1	can (4 oz.) mushroom pieces and stems, drained
½	cup chopped green pepper
1	oz. sliced pepperoni, slices cut in half (about ⅓ cup)
1	teaspoon sugar
1	teaspoon Italian seasoning, divided
½	teaspoon garlic salt

6 servings

Per Serving:
Calories:	510
Protein:	23 g.
Carbohydrate:	62 g.
Fat:	19 g.
Cholesterol:	37 mg.
Sodium:	1190 mg.
Exchanges:	3 starch,
	1 medium-fat meat,
	3½ vegetable,
	2½ fat

How to Make Herb-crusted Calzones

Heat conventional oven to 375°F. Lightly oil large baking sheet. Set aside. In large mixing bowl, combine hot roll mix, water and 2 tablespoons oil. Mix well.

Turn dough out onto lightly floured surface. Knead for 5 minutes, until smooth. Shape into ball. Cover with large bowl. Let rest for 5 minutes.

Place ground beef in 2-quart casserole. Microwave at High for 2 to 4 minutes, or until no longer pink, stirring once. Drain. Add tomato sauce, cheese, mushrooms, pepper, pepperoni, sugar, ½ teaspoon Italian seasoning and the garlic salt. Mix well. Set aside.

Cheese-stuffed Manicotti with Meat Sauce

8   uncooked manicotti shells

Filling:

1   carton (15 oz.) ricotta cheese
1   cup shredded mozzarella cheese
¼   cup grated Parmesan cheese
1   egg
¼   cup snipped fresh parsley
¼   teaspoon garlic powder

Meat Sauce:

½   lb. lean ground beef, crumbled
1   small onion, cut into thin wedges
1   large zucchini, cut in half lengthwise and sliced into ½-inch chunks (about 2 cups)
2   cups seeded chopped tomatoes
1   can (8 oz.) tomato sauce
¼   cup tomato paste
¾   teaspoon dried basil leaves
½   teaspoon sugar
¼   teaspoon garlic powder

4 servings

Prepare manicotti shells as directed on package. Rinse and drain. Set aside.

In medium mixing bowl, combine all filling ingredients. Mix well. Stuff each cooked manicotti shell evenly with cheese mixture. Set aside.

In 2-quart casserole, combine ground beef and onion. Microwave at High for 2 to 4 minutes, or until meat is no longer pink, stirring once to break apart. Drain. Add remaining meat sauce ingredients. Mix well. Cover. Microwave at High for 8 to 9 minutes, or until zucchini is tender and sauce is hot, stirring twice.

Spoon enough meat sauce into bottom of 10-inch square casserole to cover bottom. Arrange stuffed shells over sauce in casserole. Spoon remaining sauce over manicotti. Cover. Microwave at High for 11 to 13 minutes, or until hot, rotating casserole twice. Let stand, covered, for 5 minutes.

Per Serving:			
Calories:	566	Cholesterol:	157 mg.
Protein:	41 g.	Sodium:	930 mg.
Carbohydrate:	45 g.	Exchanges:	2 starch, 4 medium-fat meat,
Fat:	25 g.		3 vegetable, 1 fat

Divide dough into 6 equal portions. Roll or stretch each portion into 8 × 6-inch oval. Place ½ cup meat mixture in center of each oval.

Fold half of dough over meat mixture. Press lightly to seal edges. Place on prepared baking sheet.

Combine remaining 1 tablespoon plus 1 teaspoon oil and the remaining ½ teaspoon Italian seasoning in small bowl. Brush each calzone lightly with herb and oil mixture. Bake for 25 to 35 minutes, until lightly browned.

◄ Poor Man's Fajitas

Filling:

- ½ lb. lean ground beef, crumbled
- 1 teaspoon packed brown sugar
- ½ teaspoon dried oregano leaves
- ½ teaspoon chili powder
- ¼ teaspoon garlic powder
- ¼ teaspoon crushed red pepper flakes
- ¼ teaspoon salt
- 1 medium green pepper, cut into thin strips (4 × ¼-inch)
- 1 medium red pepper, cut into thin strips (4 × ¼-inch)
- 6 green onions, cut in half lengthwise and then crosswise
- 1 tablespoon olive oil

- 4 flour tortillas (8-inch)
  Sour cream
  Guacamole
  Salsa sauce

4 servings

In 2-quart casserole, microwave ground beef at High for 2 to 4 minutes, or until meat is no longer pink, stirring once to break apart. Drain.

Add sugar and seasonings. Mix well. Add remaining filling ingredients. Mix well. Cover. Microwave at High for 9 to 15 minutes, or until peppers are very tender, stirring twice.

Place tortillas between 2 dampened paper towels. Microwave at High for 30 seconds to 1 minute, or just until tortillas feel warm. Spoon one-fourth of meat mixture down center of each tortilla. Top with sour cream, guacamole and salsa. Roll up tortilla to enclose filling.

Per Serving:	
Calories:	251
Protein:	13 g.
Carbohydrate:	21 g.
Fat:	13 g.
Cholesterol:	37 mg.
Sodium:	248 mg.
Exchanges:	1 starch,
	1 medium-fat meat,
	1 vegetable, 1½ fat

Quick Vegetable-Beef Spaghetti

- 1 cup thinly sliced yellow summer squash
- 1 cup thinly sliced zucchini squash
- 2 tablespoons water
- 2 jars (15½ oz. each) spaghetti sauce
- 1 lb. lean ground beef, crumbled
- 1 cup frozen sliced carrots
- 1 jar (4.5 oz.) sliced mushrooms, drained
- ¼ cup red wine
- ½ teaspoon dried basil leaves
- ½ teaspoon dried oregano leaves
- 1 lb. hot cooked spaghetti

8 servings

In 3-quart casserole, combine squashes and water. Cover. Microwave at High for 3 to 5 minutes, or until tender, stirring once. Drain.

Add remaining ingredients, except spaghetti. Mix well. Cover with wax paper. Microwave at High for 20 to 25 minutes, or until meat is firm and no longer pink, stirring 3 times.

Serve over spaghetti. Sprinkle with snipped fresh parsley, if desired.

Per Serving:			
Calories:	320	Cholesterol:	35 mg.
Protein:	17 g.	Sodium:	841 mg.
Carbohydrate:	38 g.	Exchanges:	1½ starch, 1 medium-fat meat,
Fat:	11 g.		3 vegetable, 1 fat

Chimichangas

Filling:

1 lb. lean ground beef, crumbled

½ cup chopped onion

1 can (14½ oz.) diced tomatoes, drained, pressing to remove excess moisture

2 tablespoons canned chopped green chilies

2 teaspoons chili powder

1 teaspoon dried oregano leaves

½ teaspoon garlic powder

¼ teaspoon salt

Vegetable oil

8 flour tortillas (12-inch), room temperature
    Shredded lettuce
    Sour cream
    Salsa sauce

6 to 8 servings

ın 2-quart casserole, combine ground beef and onion. Mix well. Microwave at High for 4 to 7 minutes, or until meat is no longer pink, stirring once or twice to break apart. Drain. Add remaining filling ingredients. Mix well. Cover. Microwave at High for 4 to 6 minutes, or until mixture is hot and flavors are blended, stirring once or twice.

Heat ½ inch oil conventionally over medium-high heat in 10-inch deep skillet. Assemble 2 chimichangas at a time. Spoon ⅓ cup meat mixture across bottom half of tortilla, to within 1½ inches of sides. Roll up tortilla just until meat mixture is enclosed. Fold in sides and continue to roll up. Secure with wooden pick.

Place seam-sides-down in hot oil and fry until golden brown. Turn and fry other side until golden brown. Place on paper-towel-lined platter. Repeat with remaining tortillas and filling. Serve chimichangas on shredded lettuce. Top with sour cream, and salsa.

Per Serving:			
Calories:	281	Cholesterol:	35 mg.
Protein:	13 g.	Sodium:	109 mg.
Carbohydrate:	24 g.	Exchanges:	1 starch, 1 medium-fat meat,
Fat:	15 g.		2 vegetable, 2 fat

Beef, Chili & Cheese-filled Tortillas ▲

- 4 whole canned green chilies
- 2 oz. Monterey Jack cheese, cut into four 3 × 1-inch strips
- ½ lb. lean ground beef, crumbled
- 1½ cups shredded Cheddar cheese, divided
- ½ teaspoon ground cumin
- ¼ teaspoon garlic salt
- ¼ teaspoon dried oregano leaves
- 4 flour tortillas (8-inch)
- 1 envelope (0.87 oz.) white sauce mix
- 1 cup milk

4 servings

Per Serving:	
Calories:	475
Protein:	29 g.
Carbohydrate:	25 g.
Fat:	29 g.
Cholesterol:	97 mg.
Sodium:	1584 mg.
Exchanges:	1 starch,
	3 medium-fat meat,
	2 vegetable, 3 fat

How to Microwave Beef, Chili & Cheese-filled Tortillas

Place chilies on paper towel. Cut lengthwise slit in each chili. Open chilies. Remove seeds. Place 1 strip Monterey Jack cheese inside each chili. Set aside.

Place ground beef in 1-quart casserole. Microwave at High for 2 to 4 minutes, or until no longer pink, stirring once to break apart. Drain. Add 1 cup shredded Cheddar cheese, the cumin, garlic salt and oregano. Mix well.

Savory Stroganoff Crepes

Crepes:

- 2 tablespoons margarine or butter
- 1¼ cups all-purpose flour
- ¼ teaspoon salt
- 1⅓ cups milk
- 1 egg
- 2 tablespoons sour cream

Filling:

- ¾ lb. lean ground beef, crumbled
- ⅓ cup chopped onion
- ¼ cup plus 1 tablespoon all-purpose flour
- ½ teaspoon garlic powder
- ¼ teaspoon salt
- ¼ teaspoon pepper
- 1½ cups beef broth
- 1 cup sliced fresh mushrooms
- 2 tablespoons snipped fresh parsley, divided
- ⅓ cup sour cream

6 servings

In small bowl, microwave margarine at High for 45 seconds to 1 minute, or until melted. In blender, combine margarine and remaining crepe ingredients. Blend until smooth. Chill at least 1 hour.

Heat lightly oiled nonstick 6-inch skillet conventionally over medium heat. Pour 2 tablespoons batter into skillet. Tilt and swirl to coat bottom with batter. Cook about 30 seconds, or until edges begin to brown. Turn and brown other side. Repeat to yield 12 crepes. Stack crepes in single layers between sheets of wax paper. Set aside.

Heat conventional oven to 350°F. In 2-quart casserole, combine ground beef and onion. Mix well. Microwave at High for 4 to 6 minutes, or until meat is no longer pink, stirring once to break apart. Drain. Set aside.

In 4-cup measure, combine flour and seasonings. Blend in broth. Add mushrooms and 1 tablespoon parsley. Mix well. Microwave at High for 6 to 10 minutes, or until sauce thickens and bubbles, stirring every 2 minutes. Add sour cream gradually, beating with fork after each addition. Set ½ cup sauce aside.

Add remaining sauce to ground beef mixture. Mix well. Cool slightly. Spoon about 2 tablespoons mixture down center of each crepe. Roll up. Place seam-sides-down in 12 × 8-inch baking dish. Spoon reserved sauce down center. Bake 20 to 30 minutes, or until hot. Sprinkle with remaining 1 tablespoon parsley.

Per Serving:			
Calories:	353	Cholesterol:	93 mg.
Protein:	18 g.	Sodium:	498 mg.
Carbohydrate:	30 g.	Exchanges:	2 starch, 1½ medium-fat meat,
Fat:	18 g.		1 fat

Spoon one-fourth of meat mixture down center of each tortilla. Top with chilies and cheese. Roll up tortillas, enclosing meat mixture and chilies. Place tortillas seam-sides-down in 8-inch square baking dish. Set aside.

Place sauce mix in 2-cup measure. Blend in milk. Microwave at High for 3 to 5 minutes, or until mixture thickens and bubbles, stirring twice. Pour sauce evenly over tortillas.

Sprinkle with remaining ½ cup Cheddar cheese. Microwave at 70% (Medium High) for 10 to 12 minutes, or until hot and cheese is melted, rotating dish once.

Picadillo

¾ cup chopped onion
¾ cup chopped red or green
   pepper
1 tablespoon vegetable oil
½ teaspoon instant minced
   garlic
½ lb. lean ground beef,
   crumbled
1 can (14½ oz.) diced
   tomatoes, undrained
1 can (8 oz.) tomato sauce
½ cup raisins
½ cup slivered almonds
½ cup whole small pimiento-
   stuffed green olives
1 tablespoon red wine vinegar
2 teaspoons packed brown
   sugar
¼ teaspoon ground cloves
¼ teaspoon ground cumin
2 cups hot cooked long-grain
   white rice (⅔ cup uncooked)

4 servings

In 2-quart casserole, combine onion, pepper, oil and garlic. Mix well. Cover. Microwave at High for 4 to 5 minutes, or until onion and pepper are tender, stirring once.

Add ground beef. Microwave at High, uncovered, for 2 to 4 minutes, or just until meat loses pink color, stirring once to break apart.

Add remaining ingredients, except rice. Mix well. Cover with wax paper. Microwave at High for 10 to 15 minutes, or until mixture is hot and flavors are blended, stirring 2 or 3 times. Serve over rice.

Per Serving:
Calories: 476
Protein: 18 g.
Carbohydrate: 57 g.
Fat: 21 g.
Cholesterol: 35 mg.
Sodium: 954 mg.
Exchanges: 2 starch,
                 1 medium-fat meat,
                 2½ vegetable,
                 1 fruit, 3 fat

Beef & Mushroom Lasagna Roll-ups

Meat Mixture:

½ lb. lean ground beef, crumbled
1 can (14½ oz.) diced tomatoes, drained
1 cup sliced fresh mushrooms
½ cup chopped carrot
3 tablespoons tomato paste
½ teaspoon dried oregano leaves
¼ teaspoon dried thyme leaves
¼ teaspoon salt

Filling:

1 cup ricotta cheese
½ cup shredded mozzarella cheese
1 teaspoon dried parsley flakes
¼ teaspoon garlic powder

6 uncooked lasagna noodles

Sauce:

1 cup sliced fresh mushrooms
1 pkg. (0.75 oz.) mushroom gravy mix
¾ cup cold water

6 servings

In 2-quart casserole, microwave ground beef at High for 2 to 4 minutes, or until meat is no longer pink, stirring once to break apart. Drain. Add remaining meat mixture ingredients. Mix well. Cover. Microwave at High for 9 to 11 minutes, or until mushrooms are tender and mixture is slightly thickened. Set aside.

In small mixing bowl, combine all filling ingredients. Set aside. Prepare lasagna noodles as directed on package. Rinse and drain.

Spread about 2 heaping tablespoons filling on each noodle. Spread about 3 tablespoons meat mixture over filling. Set remaining meat mixture aside. Roll up each noodle, enclosing filling. Place seam-side-down in 8-inch square baking dish. Set aside.

In 1-quart casserole, combine all sauce ingredients. Mix well. Cover. Microwave at High for 4 to 6 minutes, or until sauce is thickened and translucent, stirring after first 2 minutes and then every minute. Add remaining meat mixture to sauce. Mix well.

Spoon sauce over roll-ups. Cover with wax paper. Microwave at 50% (Medium) for 10 to 17 minutes, or until hot, rotating dish 2 or 3 times.

Per Serving:			
Calories:	274	Cholesterol:	41 mg.
Protein:	18 g.	Sodium:	519 mg.
Carbohydrate:	27 g.	Exchanges:	1 starch, 1½ medium-fat meat,
Fat:	11 g.		2½ vegetable, ½ fat

Italian Pizza Singles

Crust:
1 pkg. (10 oz.) refrigerated
   pizza crust dough
   Vegetable oil or olive oil
¼ teaspoon Italian seasoning
⅛ teaspoon garlic powder

Meat Mixture:
½ lb. lean ground beef,
   crumbled
¼ teaspoon Italian seasoning
¼ teaspoon fennel seed,
   crushed (optional)
¼ teaspoon crushed red
   pepper flakes (optional)

Toppings:
½ cup spaghetti sauce
1 can (4 oz.) mushroom pieces
   and stems, drained
1 cup shredded mozzarella
   cheese
¼ cup sliced pimiento-stuffed
   green olives (optional)

4 servings

Per Serving:	
Calories:	411
Protein:	25 g.
Carbohydrate:	39 g.
Fat:	16 g.
Cholesterol:	50 mg.
Sodium:	846 mg.
Exchanges:	2 starch,
	2 medium-fat meat,
	2 vegetable, 1 fat

How to Make Italian or Mexican Pizza Singles

Heat conventional oven to 425°F. Brush large baking sheet lightly with oil. Set aside.

Remove dough from package. Unroll. Cut into four 6 × 4½-inch rectangles. Place on prepared baking sheet. Prick generously with fork.

Brush top of dough lightly with oil. Sprinkle evenly with seasonings. Bake for 8 to 10 minutes, or until golden brown. Remove to cooling rack. Set aside.

Mexican Pizza Singles

Crust:

 1 pkg. (10 oz.) refrigerated
     pizza crust dough
     Vegetable oil or olive oil
 ¼ teaspoon chili powder
 ⅛ teaspoon garlic powder

Meat Mixture:

 ½ lb. lean ground beef,
     crumbled
 ½ teaspoon chili powder
 ¼ teaspoon ground cumin

Toppings:

 ½ cup taco sauce
 1 cup shredded Cheddar
     cheese
     Shredded lettuce (optional)
 ½ cup seeded chopped tomato

4 servings

Per Serving:	
Calories:	430
Protein:	24 g.
Carbohydrate:	36 g.
Fat:	20 g.
Cholesterol:	65 mg.
Sodium:	791 mg.
Exchanges:	2 starch,
	2 medium-fat meat,
	1 vegetable, 2 fat

Place ground beef in 1-quart casserole. Microwave at High for 2 to 4 minutes, or until no longer pink, stirring once to break apart. Drain. Add seasonings. Mix well.

Spoon about 2 tablespoons sauce over each crust. Spread to within ½ inch of edges. Sprinkle evenly with meat mixture and remaining topping ingredients.

Place each pizza on individual serving plate. Microwave each pizza at High for 1 to 2 minutes, or until pizza is hot and cheese is melted, rotating once.

◄ Sukiyaki

1 lb. lean ground beef, crumbled
1 can (8 oz.) sliced water chestnuts, rinsed and drained
4 oz. fresh snow pea pods, cut into 1-inch lengths (about 1 cup)
1 cup red pepper chunks (¾-inch chunks)
4 green onions, diagonally sliced (about ½ cup)

Sauce:
1 cup chicken broth
3 tablespoons soy sauce
2 tablespoons packed brown sugar
1 tablespoon plus 1 teaspoon cornstarch
½ teaspoon ground ginger
⅛ teaspoon garlic powder
⅛ teaspoon pepper

3 cups hot cooked long-grain white rice (1 cup uncooked)

4 to 6 servings

In 2-quart casserole, microwave ground beef at High for 4 to 7 minutes, or until meat is no longer pink, stirring twice to break apart. Drain. Add water chestnuts, pea pods, pepper chunks and onions. Mix well. Set aside.

In small mixing bowl, combine all sauce ingredients. Mix well. Add to meat mixture. Cover. Microwave at High for 12 to 18 minutes, or until vegetables are tender-crisp and sauce is thickened and translucent, stirring 2 or 3 times. Serve over rice.

Per Serving:	
Calories:	334
Protein:	18 g.
Carbohydrate:	41 g.
Fat:	10 g.
Cholesterol:	47 mg.
Sodium:	692 mg.
Exchanges:	2 starch, 1 medium-fat meat, 2 vegetable, 1 fat

Ground Beef Chow Mein ▲

1 cup diagonally sliced celery (½-inch slices)
2 tablespoons water
1 lb. lean ground beef, coarsely crumbled
1 can (16 oz.) chow mein vegetables, rinsed and drained

1 jar (2 oz.) sliced pimiento, drained
1 cup beef broth
2 tablespoons soy sauce
1 tablespoon plus 1 teaspoon cornstarch
3 cups hot cooked long-grain white rice (1 cup uncooked)
¾ cup chow mein noodles

6 servings

In 2-quart casserole, combine celery and water. Cover. Microwave at High for 3 to 4 minutes, or until celery is tender-crisp, stirring once. Drain. Add ground beef. Microwave at High, uncovered, for 4 to 7 minutes, or until meat is no longer pink, stirring twice to break apart. Drain. Add vegetables and pimiento. Mix well. Set aside.

In 2-cup measure, combine broth, soy sauce and cornstarch. Mix well. Add to ground beef mixture. Mix well. Microwave at High for 9 to 14 minutes, or until mixture is thickened and translucent, stirring 3 times. Serve over rice. Sprinkle each serving evenly with chow mein noodles.

Per Serving:			
Calories:	310	Cholesterol:	47 mg.
Protein:	18 g.	Sodium:	592 mg.
Carbohydrate:	33 g.	Exchanges:	1½ starch, 1½ medium-fat meat, 2 vegetable, 1 fat
Fat:	12 g.		

One-dish Meals

English Pub Pie

1 lb. lean ground beef, crumbled
⅓ cup chopped onion
1 pkg. (1.5 oz.) beef stew seasoning mix
2 tablespoons all-purpose flour
1½ cups hot water
1 can (16 oz.) sliced potatoes, rinsed and drained

1 can (15½ oz.) diced rutabagas, rinsed and drained, or 1 can (16 oz.) julienne carrots, rinsed and drained
1 cup frozen peas
1 egg yolk
1 teaspoon water
1 sheet frozen puff pastry, defrosted (half of 17¼-oz. pkg.)

6 servings

Heat conventional oven to 400°F. In 2-quart casserole, combine ground beef and onion. Mix well. Microwave at High for 4 to 7 minutes, or until meat is no longer pink, stirring twice to break apart. Drain.

Add seasoning mix and flour. Mix well. Add 1½ cups hot water, the potatoes, rutabagas and peas. Mix well. Microwave at High for 11 to 15 minutes, or until mixture thickens and bubbles, stirring 2 or 3 times. Set aside

In small bowl, mix egg yolk and 1 teaspoon water. Set aside.

Cut puff pastry sheet to fit top of casserole. Reserve trimmings. Cut small hole in center of pastry to allow steam to escape. Fit pastry over top of casserole.

Cut leaves from reserved trimmings. Brush back sides of leaves with egg mixture. Attach to crust. Brush crust evenly with remaining egg mixture. Bake for 15 to 20 minutes, or until pastry is puffed and golden brown.

Per Serving:			
Calories:	428	Cholesterol:	94 mg.
Protein:	20 g.	Sodium:	680 mg.
Carbohydrate:	35 g.	Exchanges:	2 starch, 2 medium-fat meat,
Fat:	23 g.		1 vegetable, 2½ fat

Italian Garden Vegetable-Beef Pie ▶

1 baked and cooled deep 9-inch pastry shell
1 medium yellow summer squash, cut lengthwise into thin strips
1 medium zucchini squash, cut lengthwise into thin strips
¼ cup water
1 lb. lean ground beef, crumbled
½ cup chopped onion
¼ teaspoon instant minced garlic
1 can (8 oz.) tomato sauce
1 teaspoon dried parsley flakes
½ teaspoon ground cumin
½ teaspoon ground coriander
¼ teaspoon salt
¼ teaspoon pepper
1 medium tomato, sliced
2 tablespoons grated Parmesan cheese

6 servings

Per Serving:
Calories: 333
Protein: 17 g.
Carbohydrate: 19 g.
Fat: 21 g.
Cholesterol: 48 mg.
Sodium: 585 mg.
Exchanges: 1 starch, 2 medium-fat meat, 1 vegetable, 2 fat

How to Microwave Italian Garden Vegetable-Beef Pie

Prepare pastry shell. Set aside. In 1-quart casserole, place squash strips and water. Cover. Microwave at High for 4 to 6 minutes, or until tender, stirring gently to rearrange once. Drain. Set aside.

Combine ground beef, onion and garlic in 2-quart casserole. Mix well. Microwave at High for 4 to 7 minutes, or until meat is no longer pink, stirring twice to break apart. Drain.

Add remaining ingredients, except tomato slices and cheese, to ground beef mixture. Mix well. Spoon ground beef mixture into prepared pastry shell.

Savory Herb Stuffing Meat Pie

- 1 lb. lean ground beef, crumbled
- 1 egg
- ¼ cup unseasoned dry bread crumbs
- 1 tablespoon plus 2 teaspoons dried parsley flakes, divided
- 1 cup sliced celery
- ½ cup chopped onion
- ¼ cup margarine or butter
- ¾ cup hot water
- 3 cups cubed herb-seasoned stuffing mix
- 1 can (10¾ oz.) condensed cream of chicken soup

6 servings

In medium mixing bowl, combine ground beef, egg, bread crumbs and 1 tablespoon parsley flakes. Mix well. Pat mixture evenly into bottom of 9-inch round cake dish. Cover with wax paper. Microwave at High for 5 to 6 minutes, or until meat is firm and no longer pink, rotating dish 2 or 3 times. Drain. Set aside.

In 2-quart casserole, combine celery, onion and margarine. Cover. Microwave at High for 4 to 6 minutes, or until vegetables are tender, stirring once. Add water. Re-cover. Microwave at High for 1 to 2 minutes, or until water begins to boil. Add remaining 2 teaspoons parsley flakes and remaining ingredients. Mix well.

Spread stuffing mixture evenly over meat. Microwave at High for 2 to 5 minutes, or until hot, rotating dish once. If desired, place under conventional broiler, 4 inches from heat. Broil for 4 to 5 minutes, or until golden brown.

Arrange tomato slices in even layer over beef mixture. Arrange squash strips, alternating colors and slightly overlapping, in spoke-like fashion on top of tomato slices.

Sprinkle evenly with Parmesan cheese. Microwave at High for 6 to 8 minutes, or until pie is hot, rotating dish once.

Per Serving:	
Calories:	627
Protein:	26 g.
Carbohydrate:	60 g.
Fat:	32 g.
Cholesterol:	100 mg.
Sodium:	1613 mg.
Exchanges:	4 starch, 2 medium-fat meat, 4 fat

California Cheeseburger Pie

1 baked and cooled 9-inch
    pastry shell
1 lb. lean ground beef,
    crumbled
½ cup chopped onion
½ teaspoon seasoned salt
¼ teaspoon garlic powder
⅛ teaspoon pepper
2 cups shredded Cheddar
    cheese
½ cup mayonnaise
1 cup seeded chopped
    tomato, divided
1 cup shredded lettuce

8 servings

Prepare pastry shell. Set aside. In 2-quart casserole, combine ground beef and onion. Mix well. Microwave at High for 4 to 7 minutes, or until meat is no longer pink, stirring twice to break apart. Drain. Add seasoned salt, garlic powder and pepper. Mix well. Spoon meat mixture evenly into prepared pastry shell. Set aside.

In medium mixing bowl, combine cheese, mayonnaise and ½ cup tomato. Mix well. Spread cheese mixture evenly over ground beef mixture. Microwave pie at High for 4 to 6 minutes, or until cheese is melted, rotating pie twice.

Sprinkle lettuce around edges of pie. Mound remaining ½ cup tomato in center of pie. Garnish with dollop of mayonnaise and 1 whole black olive, if desired.

Per Serving:			
Calories:	445	Cholesterol:	73 mg.
Protein:	19 g.	Sodium:	524 mg.
Carbohydrate:	13 g.	Exchanges:	½ starch, 2 medium-fat meat,
Fat:	36 g.		1 vegetable, 5 fat

Spanish Rice & Meat Loaf

Nonstick vegetable cooking
spray
2 green pepper rings (about
¼-inch thick)
2 black olives, sliced into
8 rings
1 can (14½ oz.) diced
tomatoes, undrained
1 cup uncooked long-grain
white rice
1 cup hot water
1 can (5½ oz.) tomato juice
½ cup chopped green pepper
1 tablespoon dried parsley
flakes
3 teaspoons chili powder,
divided
1½ teaspoons paprika, divided
½ teaspoon salt
1 lb. lean ground beef,
crumbled
½ cup chopped onion
1 cup shredded Cheddar
cheese

8 servings

Spray 9 × 5-inch loaf dish with nonstick vegetable cooking spray.
Arrange pepper rings and olives in bottom of dish. Set aside.

In 2-quart casserole, combine tomatoes, rice, water, tomato juice,
pepper, parsley, 2 teaspoons chili powder, 1 teaspoon paprika and
the salt. Mix well. Cover. Microwave at High for 5 minutes. Microwave
at 50% (Medium) for 20 to 30 minutes longer, or until liquid is absorbed
and rice is tender. Let stand, covered, for 5 minutes. Fluff rice with
fork. Set aside.

In 1½-quart casserole, combine ground beef, onion, remaining 1 teaspoon chili powder and ½ teaspoon paprika. Mix well. Microwave at
High for 4 to 7 minutes, or until meat is no longer pink, stirring twice to
break apart. Drain. Add cheese. Mix well.

Spoon half of rice mixture into prepared loaf dish, packing lightly. Top
with meat mixture, packing lightly. Spoon remaining rice mixture over
meat mixture, packing lightly. Cover with plastic wrap. Microwave at
High for 3 to 5 minutes, or until hot, rotating dish once. Invert loaf onto
serving platter. Slice to serve.

Per Serving:			
Calories:	284	Cholesterol:	50 mg.
Protein:	16 g.	Sodium:	557 mg.
Carbohydrate:	26 g.	Exchanges:	1 starch, 1½ medium-fat meat,
Fat:	13 g.		2 vegetable, 1 fat

Bavarian Stuffed Cabbage

1 medium head cabbage
  (about 2 lbs.)
½ cup water

Meat Mixture:

1 lb. lean ground beef,
  crumbled
½ cup chopped onion
4 slices bacon, cut into 1-inch
  pieces
1 medium Rome apple, cored
  and cut in half lengthwise,
  divided
1 cup hot cooked long-grain
  white rice (⅓ cup uncooked)

2 tablespoons red wine vinegar
1 tablespoon packed dark
  brown sugar
¼ teaspoon salt
¼ teaspoon pepper

Sauce:

2 tablespoons packed dark
  brown sugar
2 tablespoons margarine or
  butter
1 tablespoon plus 1 teaspoon
  cornstarch
1 cup apple juice
1 tablespoon red wine vinegar

6 servings

Per Serving:			
Calories:	340	Cholesterol:	50 mg.
Protein:	17 g.	Sodium:	266 mg.
Carbohydrate:	32 g.	Exchanges:	1 starch, 1½ medium-fat meat,
Fat:	16 g.		2 vegetable, ½ fruit, 1½ fat

How to Microwave Bavarian Stuffed Cabbage

Place cabbage head and water in 2-quart casserole. Cover with plastic wrap. Microwave at High for 6 to 10 minutes, or until outer leaves are pliable, rotating dish once. Drain. Cool slightly.

Place cooled cabbage on 2 crisscrossed sheets of plastic wrap. Gently pull back pliable outer leaves (about 8 leaves). Cut out inside of cabbage, leaving outer leaves attached to stem. Set leaves aside. Chop enough cabbage to equal 1 cup. Set aside.

Combine ground beef, onion and bacon in 2-quart casserole. Microwave at High for 6 to 8 minutes, or until meat is no longer pink, stirring twice. Drain. Chop half of apple. Add to meat mixture. Set other half aside. Add chopped cabbage and remaining meat mixture ingredients to ground beef. Mix well. Set aside.

Place leaves and plastic wrap in large, deep mixing bowl. Spoon mixture into cabbage shell. Gently pull leaves toward center to enclose mixture. Secure plastic wrap tightly around cabbage. Microwave at High for 7 to 9 minutes, or until temperature in center registers 140°F. Let stand, covered, for 5 minutes.

Place 2 tablespoons brown sugar and the margarine in 1-quart casserole. Microwave at High for 45 seconds to 1 minute, or until margarine is melted. Add cornstarch. Mix well. Blend in juice and vinegar. Mix well.

Slice remaining apple half. Add to juice mixture. Microwave at High for 3 to 5 minutes, or until sauce is thickened and translucent, stirring twice. Serve cabbage in wedges. Spoon sauce over wedges.

Scandinavian Goulash

2 tablespoons margarine or butter
½ cup unseasoned dry bread crumbs
2 tablespoons snipped fresh parsley
2 cups uncooked fine egg noodles
1 lb. lean ground beef, crumbled
⅓ cup sliced green onions
1 pkg. (10 oz.) frozen peas and carrots
1 can (10¾ oz.) condensed cream of mushroom soup
¾ cup milk
½ teaspoon ground nutmeg
½ teaspoon salt
¼ teaspoon garlic powder
⅛ teaspoon pepper

6 servings

In small mixing bowl, microwave margarine at High for 45 seconds to 1 minute, or until melted. Stir in bread crumbs and parsley. Mix well. Set topping aside. Prepare noodles as directed on package. Rinse and drain. Set aside.

In 2-quart casserole, combine ground beef and onions. Mix well. Microwave at High for 4 to 7 minutes, or until meat is no longer pink, stirring twice to break apart. Drain. Set aside.

Unwrap peas and carrots and place on plate. Microwave at High for 3 to 4 minutes, or until defrosted. Drain. Add noodles, peas and carrots and remaining ingredients to meat mixture. Mix well. Cover. Microwave at High for 8 to 11 minutes, or until hot, stirring twice.

Sprinkle goulash evenly with topping. Microwave at High, uncovered, for 2 to 3 minutes, or until hot.

Per Serving:			
Calories:	358	Cholesterol:	62 mg.
Protein:	20 g.	Sodium:	791 mg.
Carbohydrate:	26 g.	Exchanges:	1½ starch, 2 medium-fat meat,
Fat:	19 g.		1 vegetable, 1½ fat

French Country Cassoulet ▶

4 slices bacon
1 lb. lean ground beef,
  crumbled
½ cup chopped onion
¼ teaspoon instant minced
  garlic
1 can (16 oz.) stewed
  tomatoes, undrained
1 can (16 oz.) great Northern
  beans, rinsed and drained
1 can (16 oz.) red kidney
  beans, rinsed and drained
2 cups frozen sliced carrots
1 can (6 oz.) tomato paste
2 tablespoons white vinegar
1 tablespoon packed brown
  sugar
1 tablespoon dried parsley
  flakes
1 teaspoon dried thyme leaves

6 to 8 servings

Layer 3 paper towels on plate. Arrange bacon on paper towels. Cover with another paper towel. Microwave at High for 3 to 6 minutes, or until bacon is brown and crisp. Set aside.

In 2-quart casserole, combine ground beef, onion and garlic. Mix well. Microwave at High for 4 to 7 minutes, or until meat is no longer pink, stirring twice to break apart. Drain.

Add remaining ingredients. Mix well. Cover. Microwave at High for 15 to 20 minutes, or until hot, stirring twice.

Arrange bacon strips in lattice pattern over top of cassoulet. Microwave at High, uncovered, for 2 to 3 minutes, or until hot.

Per Serving:	
Calories:	269
Protein:	19 g.
Carbohydrate:	29 g.
Fat:	10 g.
Cholesterol:	38 mg.
Sodium:	415 mg.
Exchanges:	1 starch, 1½ medium-fat meat, 3 vegetable, ½ fat

Hungarian Goulash

1 lb. lean ground beef,
  crumbled
½ cup chopped green pepper
⅓ cup chopped onion
1 can (16 oz.) whole tomatoes,
  undrained and cut up

1 jar (14 oz.) spaghetti sauce
1 cup frozen corn (optional)
1 cup uncooked microwave
  elbow macaroni
½ teaspoon Italian seasoning
¼ teaspoon garlic powder

6 to 8 servings

In 2-quart casserole, combine ground beef, pepper and onion. Mix well. Microwave at High for 6 to 8 minutes, or until meat is no longer pink, stirring twice to break apart. Drain.

Add remaining ingredients. Mix well. Cover. Microwave at High for 16 to 20 minutes, or until macaroni is tender, stirring every 4 minutes. Let stand, covered, for 5 minutes.

Per Serving:			
Calories:	200	Cholesterol:	35 mg.
Protein:	13 g.	Sodium:	461 mg.
Carbohydrate:	17 g.	Exchanges:	½ starch, 1 medium-fat meat,
Fat:	9 g.		2 vegetable, 1 fat

Italian Pasta & Beef Bake

8 oz. uncooked rigatoni pasta
1 cup chopped carrots
½ cup chopped onion
2 tablespoons water
1 lb. lean ground beef, crumbled
1 can (16 oz.) whole tomatoes, undrained and cut up
1 can (6 oz.) tomato paste
¼ cup red wine
½ teaspoon fennel seed, crushed
½ teaspoon dried oregano leaves
¼ teaspoon salt
3 slices (1 oz. each) Provolone cheese, cut in half

6 servings

Prepare rigatoni as directed on package. Rinse and drain. Set aside. In 3-quart casserole, combine carrots, onion and water. Cover. Microwave at High for 4 to 5 minutes, or until vegetables are tender, stirring once.

Add ground beef. Microwave at High, uncovered, for 4 to 7 minutes, or until meat is no longer pink, stirring twice to break apart. Drain.

Add rigatoni and remaining ingredients, except cheese. Mix well. Cover with wax paper. Microwave at High for 7 to 10 minutes, or until mixture is hot, stirring once.

Arrange cheese slices in circular pattern on top of pasta mixture. Place under conventional broiler, 3 inches from heat, for 4 to 7 minutes, or until cheese is golden brown and melted.

Per Serving:
Calories: 397
Protein: 24 g.
Carbohydrate: 41 g.
Fat: 15 g.
Cholesterol: 56 mg.
Sodium: 611 mg.
Exchanges: 2 starch,
2 medium-fat meat,
2 vegetable, 1 fat

Minestrone Casserole

2 tablespoons margarine or butter
¼ cup seasoned dry bread crumbs
2 tablespoons grated Parmesan cheese
1 tablespoon dried parsley flakes
1 lb. lean ground beef, crumbled
1 cup thinly sliced carrots
1 cup shredded cabbage
1 cup sliced zucchini

½ cup chopped onion
1 can (16 oz.) whole tomatoes, cut up and undrained
1 can (15 oz.) kidney beans, rinsed and drained
1½ cups hot water
1 can (8 oz.) corn, drained
1 cup uncooked microwave elbow macaroni
1 can (6 oz.) tomato paste
1 teaspoon Italian seasoning

1 teaspoon instant beef bouillon granules
½ teaspoon salt

6 servings

Per Serving:	
Calories:	428
Protein:	25 g.
Carbohydrate:	49 g.
Fat:	16 g.
Cholesterol:	49 mg.
Sodium:	856 mg.
Exchanges:	2½ starch,
	2 medium-fat meat,
	2 vegetable, 1 fat

How to Microwave Minestrone Casserole

Place margarine in small mixing bowl. Microwave at High for 45 seconds to 1 minute, or until melted. Add bread crumbs, cheese and parsley. Stir to coat with margarine. Set aside.

Combine ground beef, carrots, cabbage, zucchini and onion in 3-quart casserole. Cover. Microwave at High for 6 to 9 minutes, or just until meat loses pink color and vegetables are tender-crisp, stirring twice to break apart. Drain.

Add remaining ingredients. Mix well. Re-cover. Microwave at High for 15 to 20 minutes, or until macaroni is tender and casserole is hot, stirring twice. Sprinkle evenly with topping. Microwave at High, uncovered, for 2 to 3 minutes, or until hot.

Zucchini Lasagna*

4 medium zucchini, sliced lengthwise into ¼-inch strips
¼ cup water
1 carton (16 oz.) ricotta cheese
1 egg
¼ cup grated Parmesan cheese
1 tablespoon dried parsley flakes
1 teaspoon dried oregano leaves

1 lb. lean ground beef, crumbled
½ cup chopped onion
¼ teaspoon instant minced garlic
1 jar (15¼ oz.) spaghetti sauce
2 tablespoons all-purpose flour
2 cups shredded mozzarella cheese, divided

6 servings

* Recipe not recommended for ovens with less than 600 cooking watts.

Per Serving:	
Calories:	495
Protein:	38 g.
Carbohydrate:	23 g.
Fat:	28 g.
Cholesterol:	139 mg.
Sodium:	785 mg.
Exchanges:	1 starch, 4½ medium-fat meat, 1½ vegetable, 1½ fat

How to Microwave Zucchini Lasagna

Place zucchini strips and water in 8-inch square baking dish. Cover with plastic wrap. Microwave at High for 7 to 9 minutes, or until tender, rearranging once. Drain. Place strips on paper towels. Pat dry. Set aside.

Combine ricotta cheese, egg, Parmesan cheese, parsley and oregano in medium mixing bowl. Mix well. Set aside.

Combine ground beef, onion and garlic in 2-quart casserole. Mix well. Microwave at High for 4 to 7 minutes, or until meat is no longer pink, stirring twice to break apart. Drain. Stir in spaghetti sauce. Mix well.

Layer half of zucchini strips in 11 × 7-inch baking dish. Sprinkle evenly with 1 tablespoon flour. Spread half of ricotta cheese mixture evenly over zucchini strips.

Spoon half of meat mixture over ricotta layer. Sprinkle evenly with 1 cup mozzarella cheese. Repeat layers once, ending with meat layer.

Cover dish with wax paper. Microwave at 70% (Medium High) for 18 to 22 minutes, or until center is hot, rotating twice. Sprinkle evenly with remaining 1 cup cheese. Let stand, covered, for 10 minutes, or until cheese is melted.

Panhandler Hamburger Hash

1 lb. lean ground beef,
   crumbled
1 cup chopped green pepper
½ cup chopped onion
1 can (28 oz.) whole tomatoes,
   undrained and cut up

2 cups uncooked instant rice
2 teaspoons chili powder
½ teaspoon instant minced
   garlic
½ teaspoon salt

6 servings

In 2-quart casserole, combine ground beef, pepper and onion. Mix well.
Microwave at High for 6 to 8 minutes, or until meat is no longer pink,
stirring twice to break apart. Drain.

Add remaining ingredients. Mix well. Cover. Microwave at High for 11
to 14 minutes, or until rice is tender and liquid is absorbed, stirring 2 or 3
times. Let stand, covered, for 5 minutes. Garnish with green pepper
rings and sliced black olives, if desired.

Per Serving:
Calories:	221	Cholesterol:	47 mg.
Protein:	16 g.	Sodium:	445 mg.
Carbohydrate:	16 g.	Exchanges:	½ starch, 1½ medium-fat meat,
Fat:	11 g.		2 vegetable, ½ fat

◄ Tater-topped Hot Dish

1 lb. lean ground beef,
   crumbled
1 small onion, thinly sliced
2 cups frozen crinkle-cut
   carrots
1 cup frozen peas
1 can (10¾ oz.) condensed
   creamy onion soup
½ cup milk
1 pkg. (16 oz.) frozen potato
   nuggets

6 servings

In 8-inch square baking dish,
combine ground beef and onion.
Microwave at High for 4 to 7 minutes, or until meat is no longer
pink, stirring twice to break
apart. Drain.

Add remaining ingredients, except potatoes. Mix well. Cover
with plastic wrap. Microwave at
High for 8 to 14 minutes, or until
mixture is hot, stirring once.

Arrange potato nuggets in even
layer on top of meat mixture. Microwave at High for 5 to 6 minutes,
or until potatoes are defrosted.
Place under conventional broiler,
4 inches from heat. Broil for 4 to
6 minutes, or until golden brown.

Per Serving:
Calories:	301
Protein:	18 g.
Carbohydrate:	27 g.
Fat:	13 g.
Cholesterol:	54 mg.
Sodium:	507 mg.
Exchanges:	1 starch,
	1½ medium-fat meat,
	2½ vegetable, 1 fat

Beef & Eggplant Bake

- 1 pkg. (0.87 oz.) white sauce mix
- ¾ cup milk
- 1 lb. lean ground beef, crumbled
- 4 cups peeled cubed eggplant (½-inch cubes)
- 1 can (16 oz.) whole tomatoes, undrained and cut up
- 1 can (6 oz.) tomato paste
- ⅓ cup chopped green pepper
- 1 teaspoon dried oregano leaves
- ¼ teaspoon dried basil leaves
- ¼ teaspoon garlic powder
- ¼ teaspoon salt
- 1 cup shredded Cheddar cheese
- 2 tablespoons snipped fresh parsley

6 servings

In 2-cup measure, combine white sauce mix and milk. Mix well. Microwave at High for 2½ to 4 minutes, or until mixture thickens and bubbles, stirring every minute. Set aside.

In 8-inch square casserole, microwave ground beef at High for 4 to 7 minutes, or until no longer pink, stirring twice to break apart. Drain. Add remaining ingredients, except cheese and parsley. Mix well. Cover with plastic wrap. Microwave at High for 9 to 12 minutes, or until eggplant is tender and flavors are blended, stirring 2 or 3 times.

Spoon sauce evenly over top of eggplant mixture. Sprinkle with cheese and parsley. Microwave at High, uncovered, for 2 to 3 minutes, or until cheese is melted, rotating once. Let stand for 5 minutes.

Per Serving:

Calories:	333	Cholesterol:	69 mg.
Protein:	23 g.	Sodium:	758 mg.
Carbohydrate:	22 g.	Exchanges:	2 medium-fat meat,
Fat:	18 g.		4½ vegetable, 1½ fat

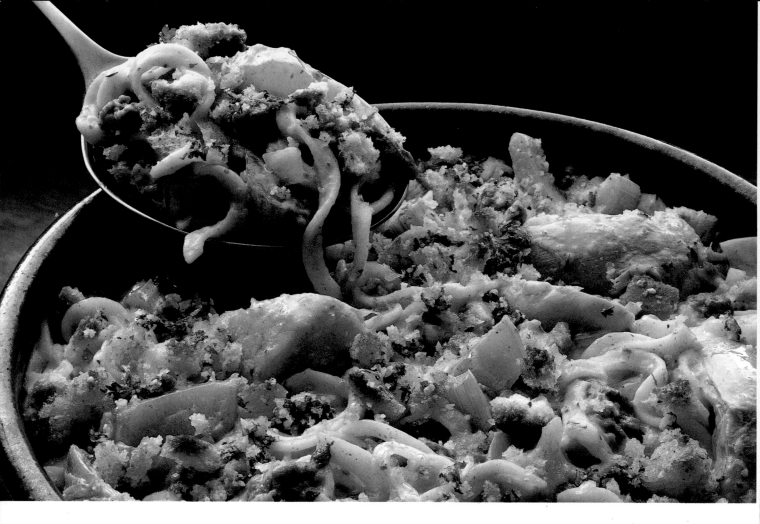

Beefy Noodle & Artichoke Casserole

2 cups uncooked medium egg noodles
1 lb. lean ground beef, crumbled
⅓ cup chopped onion
⅓ cup chopped celery
1 teaspoon Italian seasoning
2 jars (6 oz. each) marinated artichoke hearts, drained
1 can (10¾ oz.) condensed creamy onion soup
1 cup shredded Monterey Jack cheese
1 jar (2 oz.) sliced pimiento, drained

Topping:

1 tablespoon margarine or butter
1 cup garlic-seasoned croutons, coarsely crushed
2 tablespoons snipped fresh parsley
1 tablespoon grated Parmesan cheese

6 to 8 servings

Prepare noodles as directed on package. Rinse and drain. Set aside.

In 2-quart casserole, combine ground beef, onion, celery and Italian seasoning. Mix well. Microwave at High for 6 to 8 minutes, or until meat is no longer pink, stirring twice to break apart. Drain.

Add noodles and remaining ingredients, except topping. Mix well. Cover. Microwave at High for 8 to 12 minutes, or until mixture is hot, stirring twice. Set aside, covered, to keep warm.

In small mixing bowl, microwave margarine at High for 45 seconds to 1 minute, or until melted. Add remaining topping ingredients. Toss to coat with margarine. Sprinkle mixture evenly over beef and artichoke mixture. Place under conventional broiler, 4 inches from heat. Broil for 3 to 5 minutes, or until golden brown.

Per Serving:			
Calories:	301	Cholesterol:	62 mg.
Protein:	17 g.	Sodium:	539 mg.
Carbohydrate:	19 g.	Exchanges:	1 starch, 1½ medium-fat meat,
Fat:	17 g.		1 vegetable, 2 fat

Texas Beef & Corn Cake

1 lb. lean ground beef, crumbled
¾ cup chopped onion
½ cup chopped green pepper
¼ teaspoon instant minced garlic
1 can (8 oz.) tomato sauce
1 can (4 oz.) chopped green chilies, drained
1 teaspoon sugar
1 teaspoon chili powder
1 cup yellow cornmeal
⅓ cup all-purpose flour
1 teaspoon baking soda
1 teaspoon baking powder
½ teaspoon salt
2 tablespoons margarine or butter
1 can (8 oz.) corn, drained
1 cup shredded Monterey Jack cheese
1 cup milk
½ cup sour cream
1 egg
2 tablespoons honey

6 to 8 servings

Heat conventional oven to 375°F. In 10-inch square casserole, combine ground beef, onion, pepper and garlic. Microwave at High for 6 to 8 minutes, or until meat is no longer pink, stirring twice to break apart. Drain. Add tomato sauce, chilies, sugar and chili powder. Mix well. Set aside.

In large mixing bowl, combine cornmeal, flour, baking soda, baking powder and salt. Mix well. Set aside.

In small bowl, microwave margarine at High for 45 seconds to 1 minute, or until melted. Add margarine and remaining ingredients to cornmeal mixture. Blend just until moistened.

Spoon mixture evenly over meat mixture. Bake, uncovered, for 35 to 40 minutes, or until cornmeal topping is golden brown and wooden pick inserted in center comes out clean.

Per Serving:			
Calories:	387	Cholesterol:	91 mg.
Protein:	19 g.	Sodium:	739 mg.
Carbohydrate:	34 g.	Exchanges:	1½ starch, 1½ medium-fat meat,
Fat:	20 g.		2 vegetable, 2½ fat

Rio Grande Burrito Bake* ▲

6 flour tortillas (8-inch), divided
1 lb. lean ground beef, crumbled
1 can (15 oz.) chili beans in chili sauce
½ teaspoon chili powder
½ teaspoon dried oregano leaves

1 carton (12 oz.) cottage cheese
1 cup shredded Cheddar cheese
½ cup sour cream
1 can (4 oz.) chopped green chilies
1 egg
2 tablespoons all-purpose flour

6 to 8 servings

In 10-inch square casserole, arrange 4 tortillas, slightly overlapping, to cover bottom and sides of casserole. Set aside. Set aside remaining tortillas.

In 2-quart casserole, microwave ground beef at High for 4 to 7 minutes, or until no longer pink, stirring once to break apart. Drain. Add beans, chili powder and oregano. Mix well. Microwave at High for 3 to 5 minutes, or until mixture is hot and flavors are blended. Spoon meat mixture evenly into tortilla-lined casserole. Arrange remaining tortillas over mixture, cutting to fit, if necessary. Set aside.

In medium mixing bowl, combine remaining ingredients. Mix well. Spread evenly over tortillas. Cover. Microwave at 70% (Medium High) for 13 to 16 minutes, or until hot and set, rotating casserole every 4 minutes. Let stand, covered, for 5 minutes.

*Recipe not recommended for ovens with less than 600 cooking watts.

Per Serving:			
Calories:	370	Cholesterol:	106 mg.
Protein:	25 g.	Sodium:	752 mg.
Carbohydrate:	21 g.	Exchanges:	1½ starch, 3 medium-fat meat,
Fat:	21 g.		1 fat

Hamburger Gumbo Casserole

1 lb. lean ground beef, crumbled
½ cup chopped onion
½ cup red pepper strips (2 × ¼-inch)
½ cup green pepper strips (2 × ¼-inch)
¼ teaspoon instant minced garlic
1 can (16 oz.) stewed tomatoes, undrained
1½ cups uncooked 5-minute rice
1 can (10¾ oz.) condensed chicken gumbo soup
1 cup frozen peas
½ cup water
1 tablespoon dried parsley flakes
½ teaspoon salt
½ teaspoon dried oregano leaves
½ teaspoon dried thyme leaves
⅛ teaspoon cayenne

6 to 8 servings

In 2-quart casserole, combine ground beef, onion, pepper strips and garlic. Microwave at High for 6 to 8 minutes, or until meat is no longer pink, stirring twice to break apart. Drain. Add remaining ingredients. Mix well. Cover.

Microwave at High for 10 to 14 minutes, or until liquid is absorbed, rice is tender and mixture is hot, stirring twice. Let stand, covered, for 5 minutes.

Per Serving:	
Calories:	184
Protein:	13 g.
Carbohydrate:	15 g.
Fat:	8 g.
Cholesterol:	36 mg.
Sodium:	620 mg.
Exchanges:	½ starch,
	1½ medium-fat meat,
	1½ vegetable

Beef Burgundy Casserole

- 3 cups uncooked medium egg noodles
- 1 lb. lean ground beef, crumbled
- 1 cup frozen whole onions
- ¼ teaspoon instant minced garlic
- 2 cups frozen sliced carrots
- 1 jar (4.5 oz.) sliced mushrooms, drained
- 1 pkg. (1.8 oz.) oxtail soup and recipe mix
- ½ teaspoon dried marjoram leaves
- ½ teaspoon dried thyme leaves
- ¾ cup water
- ½ cup red wine
- 2 tablespoons snipped fresh parsley

6 to 8 servings

Prepare egg noodles as directed on package. Rinse and drain. Set aside.

In 2-quart casserole, combine ground beef, onions and garlic. Mix well. Microwave at High for 6 to 8 minutes, or until meat is no longer pink, stirring twice to break apart. Drain.

Add egg noodles, carrots, mushrooms, soup mix, marjoram and thyme. Mix well.

Blend in water and wine. Cover. Microwave at High for 10 to 15 minutes, or until mixture is hot and thickened, stirring twice. Sprinkle evenly with parsley.

Per Serving:
Calories:	224
Protein:	14 g.
Carbohydrate:	19 g.
Fat:	9 g.
Cholesterol:	49 mg.
Sodium:	526 mg.
Exchanges:	1 starch, 1½ medium-fat meat, 1 vegetable, ½ fat

◀ Cheesy Beef & Macaroni

    8 oz. uncooked rotelle pasta
    ½ lb. lean ground beef,
         crumbled
    ½ cup chopped red pepper
    ½ teaspoon dried oregano
         leaves
    2 pkgs. (10 oz. each) frozen
         broccoli in cheese-flavored
         sauce

                        4 to 6 servings

Prepare rotelle as directed on package. Rinse and drain. Set aside.

In 2-quart casserole, combine ground beef, pepper and oregano. Mix well. Microwave at High for 2 to 4 minutes, or until meat is no longer pink, stirring once to break apart. Drain. Set aside.

Place frozen broccoli pouches in microwave oven. Microwave at High for 3 to 6 minutes, or just until defrosted, turning pouches over once. Slit pouches and add contents to ground beef mixture. Add rotelle. Mix well. Cover. Microwave at High for 7 to 10 minutes, or until hot, stirring 2 or 3 times.

Per Serving:	
Calories:	274
Protein:	14 g.
Carbohydrate:	37 g.
Fat:	7 g.
Cholesterol:	23 mg.
Sodium:	464 mg.
Exchanges:	2 starch,
	1 medium-fat meat,
	1½ vegetable, ½ fat

Wild Rice, Asparagus & Beef Casserole

    1 tablespoon margarine or
         butter
    ¼ cup sliced almonds
    2 cups water
    ¾ cup uncooked wild rice
    2 teaspoons instant chicken
         bouillon granules
    1 lb. lean ground beef,
         crumbled
    ¼ cup chopped onion
    1 can (10¾ oz.) condensed
         cream of mushroom soup
    ½ cup sour cream
    1 pkg. (10 oz.) frozen
         asparagus cuts
    1 cup shredded Cheddar
         cheese

                            6 servings

In 9-inch pie plate, microwave margarine at High for 45 seconds to 1 minute, or until melted. Add almonds. Toss to coat with margarine. Microwave at High for 3½ to 4½ minutes, or until light golden brown, stirring every 2 minutes. Set aside.

In 2-quart saucepan, combine water, rice and bouillon. Bring to boil conventionally over high heat. Reduce heat to low. Cover. Simmer for 35 to 45 minutes, or until rice kernels are open and almost all water is absorbed. Drain. Set aside.

In 8-inch square baking dish, combine ground beef and onion. Microwave at High for 4 to 7 minutes, or until meat is no longer pink, stirring twice to break apart. Drain. Add rice, soup and sour cream to ground beef mixture. Mix well. Set aside.

Unwrap asparagus and place on plate. Microwave at High for 4 to 6 minutes, or until defrosted. Drain. Add to meat mixture. Mix well. Sprinkle evenly with cheese. Microwave at High for 8 to 14 minutes, or until hot and cheese is melted, rotating dish twice. Sprinkle evenly with almonds.

Per Serving:			
Calories:	443	Cholesterol:	76 mg.
Protein:	25 g.	Sodium:	733 mg.
Carbohydrate:	23 g.	Exchanges:	1 starch, 2½ medium-fat meat,
Fat:	28 g.		1½ vegetable, 3 fat

Baked Enchilada Salad

6 corn tortillas (6-inch), divided
  Vegetable oil
½ lb. lean ground beef,
  crumbled
1 can (14½ oz.) diced
  tomatoes, drained
½ cup taco sauce
1 teaspoon chili powder
¼ teaspoon garlic powder
¼ teaspoon salt
1 pkg. (10 oz.) frozen chopped
  spinach
1 cup sour cream
1 cup shredded Cheddar
  cheese
2 cups shredded lettuce
½ cup seeded chopped tomato

4 to 6 servings

Heat conventional oven to 400°F. Cut 3 tortillas in half. Brush 2-quart casserole lightly with oil. Place 1 whole tortilla in bottom of casserole. Stand tortilla halves, cut-sides-down, around edge of casserole, slightly overlapping. Set aside. Set remaining tortillas aside.

In medium mixing bowl, microwave ground beef at High for 2 to 4 minutes, or until meat is no longer pink, stirring once to break apart. Drain. Add canned tomatoes, taco sauce, chili powder, garlic powder and salt. Mix well. Set aside.

Unwrap spinach and place on plate. Microwave at High for 4 to 6 minutes, or until defrosted. Drain, pressing to remove excess moisture. Add to meat mixture. Mix well. In small mixing bowl, combine sour cream and cheese. Mix well.

Spoon half of meat mixture into lined casserole. Top with 1 tortilla. Spread half of sour cream mixture over tortilla. Top with remaining meat mixture and remaining tortilla. Spread remaining sour cream mixture over top.

Brush top edges of tortillas lightly with oil. Bake for 20 to 25 minutes, or until hot and bubbly. Top with shredded lettuce and chopped tomato. Serve with additional taco sauce, if desired.

Per Serving:			
Calories:	340	Cholesterol:	61 mg.
Protein:	16 g.	Sodium:	521 mg.
Carbohydrate:	22 g.	Exchanges:	1 starch, 1½ medium-fat meat,
Fat:	21 g.		1½ vegetable, 2½ fat

◄ Mock Sausage & Cheese Quiche

1 pkg. (8 oz.) refrigerated
   crescent rolls
½ lb. lean ground beef,
   crumbled
½ cup chopped green pepper
½ cup chopped onion
1 teaspoon celery salt
½ teaspoon paprika
¼ teaspoon fennel seed,
   crushed
¼ teaspoon crushed red
   pepper flakes
1 cup shredded Swiss or
   Cheddar cheese
1 can (12 oz.) evaporated milk
3 eggs
2 tablespoons all-purpose flour

6 servings

Heat conventional oven to 375°F. Remove crescent roll dough from package. Separate along perforations. Line sides and bottom of 10-inch deep-dish pie plate with dough, pressing together to seal and form crust. Bake for 10 to 12 minutes, or until golden brown. Set aside.

In 1-quart casserole, combine ground beef, green pepper and onion. Mix well. Microwave at High for 2 to 4 minutes, or until meat is no longer pink, stirring once to break apart. Drain. Add seasonings. Mix well. Spoon evenly into prepared crust. Sprinkle with cheese. Set aside.

In medium mixing bowl, combine milk, eggs and flour. Beat with whisk until smooth. Microwave mixture at 50% (Medium) for 6 to 8 minutes, or until mixture is hot and begins to set around edges, stirring with whisk every 2 minutes.

Pour egg mixture into crust. Microwave quiche at High for 2 minutes. Rotate dish. Microwave at 50% (Medium) for 8 to 12 minutes, or until set in center. Let stand for 5 minutes.

Per Serving:			
Calories:	408	Cholesterol:	196 mg.
Protein:	22 g.	Sodium:	904 mg.
Carbohydrate:	28 g.	Exchanges:	1½ starch, 2 medium-fat meat,
Fat:	23 g.		1 vegetable, 2½ fat

Ranch Burger & Bean Bake

2 slices bacon
½ lb. lean ground beef,
   crumbled
½ cup chopped onion
1 can (16 oz.) pork and beans
1 can (16 oz.) kidney beans,
   rinsed and drained
¾ cup packed brown sugar
½ cup catsup
2 tablespoons white vinegar
1 teaspoon dry mustard
2 tablespoons margarine or
   butter
1½ cups buttermilk baking mix
½ cup yellow cornmeal
1 tablespoon dried parsley
   flakes
⅔ cup milk

6 servings

Heat conventional oven to 425°F. Layer 3 paper towels on plate. Arrange bacon on paper towels. Cover with another paper towel. Microwave at High for 1½ to 2½ minutes, or until bacon is brown and crisp. Cool slightly. Crumble. Set aside.

In 2-quart casserole or soufflé dish, combine ground beef and onion. Microwave at High for 2 to 4 minutes, or until meat is no longer pink, stirring once or twice to break apart. Drain.

Add beans, sugar, catsup, vinegar and mustard. Mix well. Cover. Microwave at High for 6 to 8 minutes, or until mixture is hot, stirring twice. Set aside, covered.

In small mixing bowl, microwave margarine at High for 45 seconds to 1 minute, or until melted. Add bacon and remaining ingredients to melted margarine. Blend just until moistened. Divide mixture into sixths. Drop by spoonfuls onto top of bean mixture. Bake, uncovered, for 30 to 35 minutes, or until biscuits are deep golden brown and wooden pick inserted in center of each comes out clean.

Per Serving:			
Calories:	561	Cholesterol:	32 mg.
Protein:	20 g.	Sodium:	1022 mg.
Carbohydrate:	86 g.	Exchanges:	5 starch,
Fat:	17 g.		2 vegetable, 3 fat

Sauces, Relishes & Toppings

Mushroom Sauce

Cheesy Horseradish Sauce

- 1 tablespoon margarine or butter
- 2 tablespoons all-purpose flour
- 2 tablespoons cream-style horseradish
- 1 tablespoon stone-ground mustard
- 1 tablespoon freeze-dried chives
- 1 cup milk
- 1 cup shredded Monterey Jack cheese

1½ cups
12 servings

In 4-cup measure, microwave margarine at High for 45 seconds to 1 minute, or until melted. Stir in flour, horseradish, mustard and chives. Mix well. Blend in milk.

Microwave at High for 4 to 5 minutes, or until sauce thickens and bubbles, stirring after the first minute and then every minute. Add cheese. Stir until cheese melts. Serve as sauce with hamburgers or meatloaf.

Per Serving:			
Calories:	61	Cholesterol:	10 mg.
Protein:	3 g.	Sodium:	91 mg.
Carbohydrate:	2 g.	Exchanges:	½ vegetable,
Fat:	4 g.		1 fat

Herb Yogurt Sauce

- ¼ cup sliced green onions
- 1 tablespoon margarine or butter
- 1 teaspoon lemon juice
- ½ teaspoon freeze-dried chives
- ½ teaspoon dried parsley flakes
- ½ teaspoon dried thyme leaves
- 1 carton (8 oz.) plain low-fat yogurt
- 2 tablespoons mayonnaise

1 cup
8 servings

In 1-quart casserole, combine all ingredients, except yogurt and mayonnaise. Mix well. Cover. Microwave at High for 1½ to 3 minutes, or until onions are tender-crisp, stirring once.

Add yogurt and mayonnaise. Mix well. Serve as sauce with hamburgers or meatloaf.

Per Serving:			
Calories:	57	Cholesterol:	4 mg.
Protein:	2 g.	Sodium:	57 mg.
Carbohydrate:	2 g.	Exchanges:	½ vegetable,
Fat:	5 g.		1 fat

Curried Yogurt Sauce

½ cup finely chopped carrot
¼ cup sliced green onions
1 teaspoon margarine or butter
½ teaspoon curry powder
¼ teaspoon ground ginger
½ cup plain low-fat yogurt
1 tablespoon packed brown sugar
1 teaspoon soy sauce

1 cup
8 servings

In 1-quart casserole, combine carrot, onions, margarine, curry powder and ginger. Cover. Microwave at High for 1½ to 3 minutes, or until carrot is tender-crisp, stirring once.

Add remaining ingredients. Mix well. Serve as sauce with hamburgers or meatloaf.

Per Serving:			
Calories:	25	Cholesterol:	1 mg.
Protein:	1 g.	Sodium:	63 mg.
Carbohydrate:	4 g.	Exchanges:	1 vegetable
Fat:	1 g.		

Mushroom Sauce

8 oz. sliced fresh mushrooms (about 3 cups)
¼ cup water
2 tablespoons cornstarch
¼ teaspoon seasoned salt
1 can (10½ oz.) beef consommé

2 cups
8 servings

In 2-quart casserole, combine mushrooms and water. Cover. Microwave at High for 6 to 9 minutes, or until mushrooms are tender, stirring once. Stir in cornstarch and seasoned salt. Blend in consommé.

Microwave at High, uncovered, for 8 to 10 minutes, or until sauce is thickened and translucent, stirring 3 times. Serve as sauce with hamburgers or meatloaf.

Per Serving:			
Calories:	23	Cholesterol:	—
Protein:	2 g.	Sodium:	244 mg.
Carbohydrate:	4 g.	Exchanges:	1 vegetable
Fat:	—		

Sweet Corn & Pickle Relish ▲

½ cup chopped red pepper
½ cup chopped red onion
½ cup chopped pantry or sweet
  pickles
1 can (8 oz.) corn, drained
1 tablespoon vegetable oil
½ cup sugar

⅓ cup white vinegar
1 tablespoon mustard seed
½ teaspoon celery seed
¼ teaspoon garlic powder
¼ teaspoon crushed red
  pepper flakes

2 cups
16 servings

In small mixing bowl, combine pepper, onion, pickles, corn and oil.
Set aside.

In 2-cup measure, combine remaining ingredients. Mix well. Microwave
at High for 1½ to 2 minutes, or until sugar is dissolved, stirring twice.

Pour over corn mixture. Toss to coat. Cover and refrigerate overnight
to blend flavors. Store in refrigerator, covered, no longer than 2 weeks.
Serve as relish with hamburgers or meatloaf.

Per Serving:			
Calories:	57	Cholesterol:	—
Protein:	1 g.	Sodium:	78 mg.
Carbohydrate:	12 g.	Exchanges:	2 vegetable
Fat:	1 g.		

Jicama Salsa

2 cups seeded chopped
  tomato
1 cup chopped jicama
½ cup sliced green onions
2 tablespoons canned
  chopped green chilies
1 tablespoon red wine vinegar
½ teaspoon dried cilantro
  leaves
¼ teaspoon salt
¼ teaspoon pepper

3 cups
6 servings

In medium mixing bowl, combine
all ingredients. Mix well. Cover
and refrigerate overnight to blend
flavors. Serve as relish with hamburgers or meatloaf.

Per Serving:	
Calories:	28
Protein:	1 g.
Carbohydrate:	6 g.
Fat:	—
Cholesterol:	—
Sodium:	136 mg.
Exchanges:	1 vegetable

Winter Chow-Chow

Dressing:
- 2 tablespoons white vinegar
- 2 tablespoons olive oil
- 2 teaspoons sugar
- ½ teaspoon celery seed
- ¼ teaspoon salt
- ⅛ teaspoon ground turmeric
- 5 drops red pepper sauce

- ½ cup small fresh cauliflowerets
- ½ cup sliced celery
- ½ cup chopped red pepper
- ¼ cup water
- 1 jar (6 oz.) marinated artichoke hearts, drained and coarsely chopped
- ½ cup coarsely chopped seeded cucumber
- ½ cup sliced black olives

2½ cups
18 servings

In 1-cup measure, combine all dressing ingredients. Mix well. Set aside.

In 2-quart casserole, combine cauliflowerets, celery, pepper and water. Cover. Microwave at High for 4 to 6 minutes, or until vegetables are tender-crisp, stirring once. Drain.

Add remaining ingredients and the dressing. Mix well. Cover and refrigerate overnight to blend flavors. Store in refrigerator, covered, no longer than 2 weeks. Serve as relish with hamburgers or meatloaf.

Per Serving:
Calories:	34
Protein:	—
Carbohydrate:	2 g.
Fat:	3 g.
Cholesterol:	—
Sodium:	83 mg.
Exchanges:	½ vegetable, ½ fat

Lemon Pesto Topping ▲

¼ cup chopped fresh basil
  leaves
1 tablespoon finely chopped
  onion
1 tablespoon olive oil
2 cloves garlic, minced
1 teaspoon grated lemon peel
¾ cup mayonnaise or salad
  dressing
2 teaspoons prepared mustard

¾ cup
12 servings

In 1-quart casserole, combine basil, onion, oil, garlic and lemon peel. Mix well. Cover. Microwave at High for 1 to 1½ minutes, or until onion is tender-crisp, stir-ring once.

Add mayonnaise and mustard. Mix well. Store in refrigerator, cov-ered, no longer that 1 week. Serve as topping with hamburgers or meatloaf.

Per Serving:	
Calories:	112
Protein:	—
Carbohydrate:	1 g.
Fat:	12 g.
Cholesterol:	8 mg.
Sodium:	91 mg.
Exchanges:	2½ fat

Jalapeño Honey Mustard

¾ cup chopped onion
3 whole canned jalapeño
  peppers, chopped (about
  3 tablespoons)
2 cloves garlic
½ cup prepared mustard
2 tablespoons honey
1 tablespoon packed dark
  brown sugar

¾ cup
12 servings

In 1-quart casserole, combine onion, peppers and garlic. Mix well. Cover. Microwave at High for 4 to 6 minutes, or until onion is tender, stirring once.

In food processor or blender, combine onion mixture and re-maining ingredients. Process until smooth.

Spoon mustard into sterilized jar. Store in refrigerator, covered, no longer than 2 weeks. Serve as topping with hamburgers or meatloaf.

Per Serving:	
Calories:	28
Protein:	1 g.
Carbohydrate:	6 g.
Fat:	—
Cholesterol:	—
Sodium:	126 mg.
Exchanges:	1 vegetable

Tomato-Garlic Mayonnaise

1 cup mayonnaise
1 tablespoon tomato paste
¼ cup water
4 cloves garlic, peeled

1 cup
16 servings

In small mixing bowl, combine mayonnaise and tomato paste. Mix well. Set aside.

In 1-cup measure, place water and garlic. Cover with plastic wrap. Microwave at High for 1 to 1½ minutes, or until water boils. Remove garlic from water. Mash with fork.

Add to mayonnaise mixture. Mix well. Cover. Refrigerate overnight to blend flavors. Store in refriger-ator, covered, no longer than 2 weeks. Serve as topping with hamburgers or meatloaf.

Per Serving:	
Calories:	102
Protein:	—
Carbohydrate:	1 g.
Fat:	11 g.
Cholesterol:	8 mg.
Sodium:	88 mg.
Exchanges:	2 fat

Blue Cheese Burger Topping

1 pkg. (3 oz.) cream cheese
¼ cup sour cream
¼ cup crumbled blue cheese
3 tablespoons milk
1 clove garlic, minced
1 teaspoon brandy (optional)

¾ cup
6 servings

In small mixing bowl, microwave cream cheese at 50% (Medium) for 30 seconds to 1 minute, or until softened. Add remaining ingredients. Mix well. Serve as topping with hamburgers or meatloaf.

Per Serving:			
Calories:	95	Cholesterol:	25 mg.
Protein:	3 g.	Sodium:	130 mg.
Carbohydrate:	2 g.	Exchanges:	2 fat
Fat:	9 g.		

Red Pepper Mayonnaise

½ large red pepper (about 4 oz.)
¾ cup mayonnaise

¾ cup
14 servings

Place pepper half cut-side-down in 8-inch square baking dish. Cover with plastic wrap. Microwave at High for 4 to 6 minutes, or until tender, rotating dish once.

Place pepper in cold water until cool. Remove and discard skin. Drain pepper on paper towels.

In food processor or blender, process pepper until smooth (about ¼ cup). Add mayonnaise to puréed pepper. Mix well. Store in refrigerator, covered, no longer than 1 week. Serve as topping with hamburgers or meatloaf.

Per Serving:	
Calories:	88
Protein:	—
Carbohydrate:	1 g.
Fat:	10 g.
Cholesterol:	7 mg.
Sodium:	68 mg.
Exchanges:	2 fat

Smoky Sweet Hot Catsup

1 can (28 oz.) whole tomatoes, drained
1 can (12 oz.) tomato paste
1 can (8 oz.) tomato sauce
⅓ cup packed brown sugar
1 tablespoon prepared mustard
2 teaspoons instant minced onion
½ teaspoon garlic powder
½ teaspoon ground cinnamon
¼ teaspoon cayenne
¼ teaspoon mesquite liquid smoke flavoring

4 cups
32 servings

In 2-quart casserole, combine all ingredients. Mix well, stirring to break apart tomatoes. Cover. Microwave at 70% (Medium High) for 18 to 22 minutes, or until flavors are blended and mixture is desired consistency, stirring twice. Let cool for 1 hour.

Spoon catsup into sterilized jar. Store in refrigerator, covered, no longer than 2 weeks. Serve as topping with hamburgers or meatloaf.

Per Serving:	
Calories:	25
Protein:	1 g.
Carbohydrate:	6 g.
Fat:	—
Cholesterol:	—
Sodium:	135 mg.
Exchanges:	1 vegetable

Southwestern Catsup

2 tomatoes, peeled, seeded and chopped (about 2 cups)
1 can (4 oz.) chopped green chilies, undrained
½ cup chopped green pepper
⅓ cup chopped onion
2 large cloves garlic, minced
1 tablespoon packed brown sugar
1 tablespoon vegetable oil
½ teaspoon chili powder
1 can (8 oz.) tomato sauce
1 can (6 oz.) tomato paste
1 tablespoon red wine vinegar
1 teaspoon Worcestershire sauce

3½ cups
28 servings

In 2-quart casserole, combine tomatoes, chilies, pepper, onion, garlic, sugar, oil and chili powder. Mix well. Cover. Microwave at High for 10 to 12 minutes, or until onion and pepper are tender, stirring twice.

Add remaining ingredients. Mix well. Cover with wax paper. Microwave at High for 10 to 12 minutes, or until flavors are blended and mixture is desired consistency, stirring 2 or 3 times.

Spoon catsup into sterilized jar. Store in refrigerator, covered, no longer than 2 weeks. Serve as topping with hamburgers or meatloaf.

Per Serving:	
Calories:	19
Protein:	1 g.
Carbohydrate:	3 g.
Fat:	1 g.
Cholesterol:	—
Sodium:	148 mg.
Exchanges:	½ vegetable

Italian or Mexican Pizza Singles (pages 110 and 111)
Cantaloupe Wedges

Cut cantaloupe into wedges; cover and refrigerate until serving time. Heat conventional oven and bake pizza crust. While pizza crusts are baking, prepare pizza topping. Assemble pizzas.

Menus

Speedy Lunches

Adults as well as children will enjoy these easy, well-balanced lunches. The Alphabet Beef Soup menu can be packed as a take-along lunch and reheated in a microwave oven.

> **Alphabet Beef Soup (page 65)**
> **Crackers & Cheese**
> **Green Apple Slices**
>
> Prepare and microwave soup. Slice apple and cheese and arrange on serving platter with crackers.

> **Open-face Vegetable-Beef**
> **Sandwich (page 47)**
> **Fresh Fruit**
>
> Prepare fruit. Cover and chill until ready to serve. Prepare sandwich topping; assemble sandwiches, and microwave.

Rush-hour Menus

After a busy day, and before an equally busy evening, you need a simple, easy-to-prepare family menu. Make these hearty meals quickly with ingredients you keep on hand or can have available with a minimum of planning.

**California Cheeseburger Pie
 (page 118)
Catsup, Pickles & Relishes**

Heat conventional oven and bake pastry shell. Microwave pie filling. Serve with condiments.

**Barbecue-topped Corn Muffins
 (page 45)
Deli Coleslaw
Watermelon Slices**

Microwave barbecue beef mixture. Cut muffins into quarters and place on individual serving plates. Slice watermelon. Spoon barbecue beef mixture over muffins. Serve with coleslaw.

**Quick Vegetable-Beef
  Spaghetti (page 104)
Mixed Green Salad
Garlic Bread**

Prepare spaghetti sauce. While
sauce is microwaving, cook pasta
conventionally. Prepare salad
and bread.

**Shepherd's Stuffed Potatoes
  (pages 98 and 99)
Tossed Green Salad
Sliced Fresh Fruit**

Assemble and chill salad. Slice
fruit. Cover and chill until serving
time. Microwave potatoes while
preparing ingredients for potato
filling. Stuff potatoes. Toss salad
with dressing.

Light & Easy Meals

For the warm days of spring and summer, or any time the family prefers a light meal, these menus are quick and easy to prepare.

The Mock Sausage & Cheese Quiche menu may be served as a light evening meal or a brunch for entertaining guests.

Santa Fe Salad (page 29)
Red & Green Grapes

Heat conventional oven and bake salad shells as directed on package. While salad shells bake, prepare salad filling in microwave. Serve with grapes.

Mock Sausage & Cheese
  Quiche (page 137)
Assorted Muffins
Bibb Lettuce tossed with
  Strawberries & Bananas

Prepare quiche. Heat muffins in
conventional oven and assemble
salad while microwaving quiche.

Hamburger Steaks with
  Vegetable Salsa (page 93)
Honeydew Melon & Raspberries
Bread Sticks

Prepare fruit. Cover and chill until
ready to serve. Prepare vegetable
salsa. Set aside, covered, to keep
hot. Microwave hamburger
steaks. Serve with bread sticks.

Entertaining in an Hour

These menus take less than an hour to prepare, but they're festive enough for a party. Choose one of these entrées for a spur-of-the-moment party or occasions when you want to fit entertaining into a very busy schedule.

Zucchini Lasagna (page 126)
Romaine Salad tossed with
 Mandarin Oranges
French Bread

Prepare and chill salad. Warm bread in conventional oven. Assemble lasagna, and micro-wave. Toss salad.

Cincinnati Chili (page 51)
Light Green Salad
Fresh Fruit

Assemble and chill salad. Prepare fruit; cover and refrigerate until serving time. Cook spaghetti con-ventionally. Prepare and micro-wave chili. Toss salad with dressing.